SINGLE AND LOVING IT

SINGLE AND LOVING IT

Living Life to the Fullest

by

Kate McVeigh

Harrison House
Tulsa, Oklahoma

11 10 09 08   18 17 16 15 14 13 12 11

Single and Loving It—
Living Life to the Fullest
ISBN 13: 978-1-57794-440-9
ISBN 10: 1-57794-440-2
Copyright © 2003 by Kate McVeigh
Kate McVeigh
P.O. Box 1688
Warren, MI 48090
www.katemcveigh.org

Published by Harrison House, Inc.
P.O. Box 35035
Tulsa, Oklahoma 74153

Contents

INTRODUCTION

One day a friend called me on the phone, and she was crying.

"Kate!" she sobbed. "I'm still single and I don't feel like I will *ever* be married! Why haven't I met anybody? It seems like everyone else is married, and all the good men are taken. If I finally *do* meet a good-looking guy who has his act together, it turns out he's not saved!" She finished in a hurt voice, "I feel like God doesn't care about me at all."

Have you ever felt that way? My friend is a very attractive Christian girl and she has a lot of things going for her, yet she's still unmarried. I meet so many Christian singles who feel exactly like she did that day—like God has forgotten about them or doesn't care about how much they want to find someone to spend their lives with.

You may be divorced, widowed, a single parent, or maybe you're like me and you've never been married. No matter what category you may fall into, God does care about you! He has a great plan for your life no matter where you've been or what you're going through now. I want you to know that it's worth waiting for the one whom God has for you!

Jeremiah 29:11 (NIV) says, "'For I know the plans I have for you,' declares the Lord, 'plans to prosper you and not to harm you, plans to give you hope and a future.'" Your future is bright! As a matter of fact, it's so bright you're going to have to put on sunglasses!

My prayer is that as you read this book, it will be a life-changing experience for you. While you are in this season of singleness, make the best of it by drawing near to God and getting to know Him better. Take advantage of this time you have right now to focus all your attention on Him. This book will help give you the tools you need to be an uncommon single and soar with God, being all you were created to be.

Get ready to triumph and live an uncommon, victorious, exceptional Christian life!

1

SINGLE
AND
SUCCESSFUL

1

SINGLE AND SUCCESSFUL

God wants you to be successful! Your success in life is not based on your marital status. Just because you are single does not mean you cannot be successful.

Being single also does not mean you are incomplete. Some people think the definition of the word *single* means "alone," but that's not really what it means.

Strong's Exhaustive Concordance of the Bible defines "single" in the Greek "...as a particle of union...."[1] W. E. Vine defines it as, "...simple..." and "...simplicity...."[2] And the root of the word *singular* in the Hebrew means, "to separate or distinguish, to make great or wonderful."[3]

Webster's definitions of the word *single* include: "...consisting of a separate unique whole...unbroken, undivided...having no equal or like...a separate individual or thing...."[4]

> *You don't have to be married to be whole...you are already complete in Christ.*

Notice it says "a separate unique whole." That means you don't have to be married to be a whole person. God says in His Word that if you are a Christian, you are complete in Jesus Christ. You are already whole and complete in Him.

> *And ye are complete in him, which is the head of all principality and power.*

Colossians 2:10

As far as God is concerned, you can be single and successful! A big part of being successful is following His plan for your life and obeying Him. Being in the will of God is a big key in being successful.

It is important that we do not compare ourselves to others—we have to follow God's plan for our own individual lives. We all have our own unique path to follow—we're not all called to do the same thing. If we were, how boring that would be! For example, if I were to compare myself with my friends, I could get discouraged, because most of them are married and have children.

Don't sit in your **setback,** *but do your part in God's* **comeback** *plan for your life!*

From early on I sensed that it would be awhile before I got married. I felt the Lord leading me to get my ministry established before settling down. Looking back now I can see the wisdom in waiting, because in the pioneering stage, a traveling ministry is a lot of work, and I had to be gone all the time and give up a lot of freedom.

Now that I'm more established, if I were to get married, I could pick and choose when and where I want to go.

Make Yourself Valuable

Everyone, whether married or single, should make it their goal to become as valuable as they possibly can. You should become so valuable that if you were to move, the people around you would miss you terribly and cry over your leaving! You don't want them to celebrate!

You can devote more time to sharpening your skills and developing your gifts, talents, and abilities while you are single.

Don't Sit in Your Setback

I have a friend who chose not to sit in her setback, but do her part in God's comeback plan for her life. Maybe you've had a setback and now you find yourself single. Or maybe you're single and you just find *that* to be a setback!

My friend had a severe setback when her husband passed away very suddenly at thirty-seven years of age, leaving her with two young sons and a church. She could have allowed herself to be overcome with questions, grief, or fear, wondering if God really is good. But she didn't let herself go there. Instead, she acted on God's Word and trusted Him completely.

Every time I called her, she spoke only words of faith concerning her situation. She ministered comfort to her congregation and to me. She refused to let the devil get her down and believed that the Lord would turn this negative situation into something positive. She didn't sit in her setback and feel sorry for herself, even though she could have.

She ran the church successfully for several years, developing her gifts and becoming more and more valuable. Now she travels around teaching other people how to raise their children and helping them to overcome hard situations by trusting the Lord. She also developed her writing and administrative skills, and she has helped me on many projects. She is a great blessing. She has become very valuable and is sought after by many people. Being single didn't hold her back from becoming all she could be in God.

You can do as she did and hold fast to the Word of God. Make it your goal to be single and *successful* in this season of your life!

2
DON'T
BE
DISCOURAGED

2

DON'T BE DISCOURAGED

Have you ever felt as though the whole world revolves around married people? I know I have. Sometimes the devil may try to make you feel as if you're less of a person because you don't have a mate. He'll try to make you feel inferior, as if you've been put on a shelf and forgotten.

Discouragement comes knocking on everyone's door at one time or another, and it seems as if that's especially true with singles. But don't be discouraged; God has not forgotten you! The Bible tells us that He's always working on His plan for your life.

Being confident of this very thing, that he which hath begun a good work in you will perform it until the day of Jesus Christ.

Philippians 1:6

Faithful is He who calls you, and He also will bring it to pass.

1 Thessalonians 5:24 NASB

And we know that all things work together for good to them that love God, to them who are the called according to his purpose.

Romans 8:28

God knows how you're feeling and what it's like to be lonely at times. Just hang in there because His Word is working, and His best is yet to come in your life!

Make God Your Source

It's important to always remember that true joy comes from God alone and not just from being married.

Ye are of God, little children, and have overcome them: because greater is he that is in you, than he that is in the world.

1 John 4:4

When we are aware of who lives on the inside of us, we can banish discouragement about being single. I want to encourage you to make God your Source. He wants to be your total Source of joy and security.

I'd rather be single and happy than married to the wrong one and be miserable!

The Lord is my light and my salvation; whom shall I fear? the Lord is the strength of my life; of whom shall I be afraid?

Psalm 27:1

We must continually remind ourselves that our security and confidence come from *who* we are in Christ, not in what we *do* or even to whom we're married. We must focus on becoming secure in God, because if we're insecure and we end up with someone who's insecure, we just end up with two insecure people married to each other!

There are a lot of single people who think that being married is the answer to all their problems, but it isn't. We all probably know married people who could testify to that fact.

I always say this: I'd rather be single and happy, than married to the wrong one and be miserable! I've known people who became overly anxious about getting married and just settled for less than God's best. (We'll talk more about that in chapter four.)

Purpose in your heart not to settle for second best, but wait for God's best no matter how long it takes.

There were many great people throughout history who were single. Jesus was single! As far as we know, the apostle Paul was single, and Daniel was single. There have been a lot of great men and women of faith who weren't married and served the Lord with excellence. Whether you want to be married or not, you can still serve the Lord with excellence right where you are by seeking Him first and putting your faith in Him.

Rejoice Over the Blessings of Others

Most of my friends are married, and I've been to a lot of weddings. I've even been in them, but none of them have been my own! Now *that* could be discouraging. When you see someone else getting blessed and marrying the person of their dreams, it can be a little tempting to feel jealous. Purpose in your heart that you will not yield to those feelings. Look at what the Bible says to do.

Rejoice with them that do rejoice, and weep with them that weep.

Roman 12:15

Please know that just because you have a thought of jealousy doesn't mean you have sinned. It's when you yield to those thoughts that you get into trouble. It's just like resisting any other thing that tries to attack you, such as sickness or poverty. You resist it at its onset.

...Resist the devil [stand firm against him], and he will flee from you.

James 4:7 AMP

If you want to be married, then you're not one of those called to be single.

We're to resist him *immediately!* In other words, do not wait until jealousy sets in to such a degree that it becomes a stronghold. Rebuke it now.

Simply say, "Jealousy, I rebuke you in the name of Jesus. I refuse to be jealous. I will rejoice over the blessings of others, and as I do, the Lord will bless me too."

"Am I Called To Be Single?"

I've met a lot of single people who ask me, "What if I'm called to be single? What if I'm one of those?" And they say it with a little bit of fear in their voice.

I just want you to know that if you *want* to be married, *then you're not one of those!* God wants to give you the desires of your heart.

And it's never too late. Some people think they're too old to get married, but it's not true. One time an 84-year-old man asked me to pray with him for a wife. At first I thought he was joking! But that was really the desire of his heart.

So I said, "Sure, if that's the desire of your heart, then God will give it to you. I'll pray with you!" We prayed, and do you know it wasn't too long after that, that God brought him a beautiful wife, and they have a wonderful relationship. She was 75, and he told me later that he married a younger woman! God can give you the desire of your heart, too, no matter how old you are or what your circumstances may be.

Don't Be Afraid

Every time I talk to a group of singles, there is always someone who says they don't want to be married. And that's fine, as long as you want to be single for the right reason. But sometimes people want to remain single out of fear and not because the Lord is leading them to be single.

When a relationship in the past has gone sour, we're often afraid to try again.

If it's your heart's desire to be married, then you can stand on God's Word knowing that He will bring it to pass.

Too many times our lives are about "failure avoidance." We're so afraid of failure and rejection that we determine never to get married because we don't want to be hurt again. I've known many people who put walls up because they've been hurt in the past, saying, "I will *never* be involved in a relationship again." Really they're saying that out of fear, and they may be closing the door to a better plan for their life.

I often ask these people, "Would you get married if you found the right person?" and they almost always say yes. So I want to encourage you to examine your heart and not be afraid to believe God for a mate.

Delight thyself also in the Lord; and he shall give thee the desires of thine heart.

Psalm 37:4

God wants to give you the desires of your heart, and that includes a mate. If it's your heart's desire to be married, then you can stand on God's Word knowing that He will bring it to pass.

But notice what this Scripture says that we should do first, and that is to delight ourselves in the Lord. In other words, we should not allow our thinking to be so consumed with wanting to be married that we miss what God has for us in this season of our life. Because you know what? You can never go back in time. So enjoy the season that you're in right now, and keep pressing into God.

Don't Wait for Your Mate To Get Busy With Your Vision

A lot of people I know have put their life on hold, waiting for the person they're going to marry. They may feel called to the ministry, called to start their own business, or called to help in a certain place in their church, but they don't take the step because they're *waiting* for a mate before they start. In other words, they're not going to do anything about fulfilling their vision until they get married.

I liken that to the Rapture. We know that Jesus is going to return and that the Rapture is going to take place some time, but we have to prepare in the natural realm as though He's not. For example, we still put money aside in savings for retirement, even though it's possible that we may not even be here. We must keep on living and preparing for our future.

We need to live our single life as though we're never going to get married, but we believe that we are. Live your life and prepare for things as if you might not get married, even though you know you will. We're to live like Jesus is coming tomorrow, but we have to prepare as though He may not come in our lifetime.

Don't wait to do the things that God has put in your heart—get busy fulfilling your vision.

For example, I bought a house when I was very young. Sure, I'd rather have a house with a husband, but since he's not here yet, I thought it would be wise to have an investment. I also save money every month, and I have a retirement account, preparing for the future as though I won't be married. (But I believe I will!) This is not a lack of faith, as some people would have you believe—it's just smart!

I didn't wait for a mate to start preaching the Gospel all around the world. I went to Bible college right after high school, and it seemed as if everyone I knew met their husband there, got married, and left to go into the ministry together. Everyone, that is, except me!

So I said, "Lord, I'm just going to take advantage of this time." I knew that God had called me to preach, and from that time to this, I have been able to travel and preach all over the world. But that's because I focused my purpose and my attention on fulfilling the call of God on my life and doing what He has called me to do.

Looking back on it now, I can see that I may never have been able to do many of the things I've done if I had gotten married right away. I can see God's wisdom in having me wait a little longer.

Get Busy

So don't wait to do the things that God has put in your heart—get busy fulfilling your vision. Start doing what God has for you to do. If you're not sure what God has for you to do, then I encourage you to get involved in your local church.

That's what I did in the beginning. I worked in children's ministry for five years when I first got saved. There was a need, so I helped to fill it. As I worked for the Lord, my calling became more clear. You don't always start out where you may end up. A lot of times people won't help in an area because they're not sure if that's what God has for them, so they do nothing! I have found that once people get busy doing something for the Lord and being faithful, then promotion comes.

When you bless people in your church, you are really blessing God Himself, and you cannot out give God. The book of Hebrews talks about how God rewards those who serve in the local church.

> *For God is not unrighteous to forget or overlook your labor and the love which you have shown for His name's sake in ministering to the needs of the saints (His own consecrated people), as you still do.*
>
> Hebrews 6:10 AMP

Focus on being a blessing and what God has called you to be, and then everything else in your life—like getting married—will fall into place.

God is ordering your steps and preparing the right mate for you. So it's really important that you watch your words and agree with Him.

Enjoy This Season

If it's our desire to be married, and we know God wants to give us the desire of our hearts, then we know that we are single only for a *season.* So we might as well enjoy this season!

To be able to enjoy this season, we must get into faith instead of being anxious. I believe, friend, that God is ordering your steps and preparing the right mate for you. So it's really important that you watch your words and *agree with Him*. Words are powerful! They are like containers. They carry power.

> *Death and life are in the power of the tongue: and they that love it shall eat the fruit thereof.*

Proverbs 18:21

That means we need to stop saying things like, "I don't know if I'll ever get married!" Instead, we should speak words of faith over our lives.

I remember one day when I was feeling sorry for myself. (I know you've never been there!) The devil was reminding me of all the people who were married and reminding me that I had nobody. Has that ever happened to you? So I turned on the TV and I saw a preacher who, right when I tuned in, just happened to be saying, "Stop your bawling, squalling, and crying!" I'll tell you, he jerked the slack right out of me!

You and I must realize the source of our discouragement and do what Jesus did about it. He spoke to it!

And I realized something at that moment. God cares about my feelings and the struggles that I'm going through, and that means He cares about you, too. But the only way something is going to *change* in our lives is by our *faith!*

Whether we like it our not it's our faith, not our tears, that changes circumstances.

So that day I purposed in my heart not to be caught in the trap of self-pity and depression, but to believe that God is working behind the scenes.

Speak to Discouragement

All of us have had opportunities to get discouraged, as I mentioned before. Even Jesus Himself was tempted to be discouraged. In Matthew 16 Jesus told the disciples how He was going to go to the cross and suffer the most horrible death any human being ever suffered. Now *that* could be discouraging.

Right at that moment, Peter stuck his foot in his mouth.

> *Then Peter took him, and began to rebuke him, saying, Be it far from thee, Lord: this shall not be unto thee.*

> Matthew 16:22

In the Greek translation of this verse, Peter is literally saying to Jesus, "Pity thyself."[1] In other words, Peter was trying to get Jesus to feel sorry for Himself. Actually, it wasn't Peter; it was the devil himself. He is the source behind all discouragement.

You and I must realize the source of our discouragement and do what Jesus did about it. And that is, He spoke to it! He spoke to discouragement. In verse 23 He said, "…Get thee behind me, Satan…." Whenever self-pity tries to come your way, be like Jesus and command it to leave your life.

Your words are very powerful. After you speak to discouragement, you can start saying, "I believe I'm full of joy," because Proverbs 15:23 says, "A man hath joy by the answer of his mouth...." Even your level of joy is determined by the words that you speak.

Don't Worry, Be Happy

You can trust that God is ordering and directing your life. Maybe you're single right now and that's not what you want, but that's where God has you. You can say, "Lord, there must be a purpose in this, so I'm going to take advantage of this season. And I'm going to minister to people and be a blessing."

> The steps of a good man [or woman] are ordered by the Lord: and he delighteth in his way.
>
> Psalm 37:23

Sometimes we're waiting for that special place in our life to be happy, but we need to learn to enjoy every phase of our life NOW.

If that verse is true (and it is!), then we can enjoy this season of being single.

Now, a lot of people think that Scripture says, "Our *leaps* are ordered of God"! Have you ever wanted God to order your leaps? I have! I've wanted to go from one place to the next and be there NOW! But He does things in steps, not in leaps.

If you're not careful, you can allow the devil to discourage or depress you because it seems to be taking too long, and then you begin to turn inward. A lot of times we start to think only of ourselves because there's no one else around to think of. Then we become consumed and concerned with only ourselves. If we're not careful, it's very easy for single people to become selfish.

We need to reach out to other people and not allow ourselves to wallow in self-pity. Just because you're single doesn't mean you're not whole. You can still be single, sanctified, and satisfied! This might be a revelation to you, but *you can be single and happy at the same time!*

Many single people think, *When I get married, then I'll be happy.* But they get married and they're still not happy! So they think, *Well, when we have kids, then I'll be happy.* They have kids and they're still not happy, so they say, *When the kids move out, then I'll be happy!* And then the kids move out and they're *still* not happy.

Sometimes we're waiting for that special place in our life to be happy, but we need to learn to enjoy *every* phase of our life *NOW.* God has you here right now for a reason, so enjoy it!

I remember one time I was having lunch with a very well-known minister of God and she said to me, "Kate, looking back over my life, if I could do anything differently, I would learn to enjoy every single phase of my ministry."

You see, a lot of times we're not happy in each phase of our life because we're waiting for the next one to come. So we have to purpose in our hearts to be happy right where we are. That means enjoying where we are on the way to where we're going!

There Are Advantages To Being Single

As singles, we can be a big blessing to our church and to the kingdom of God.

While you're in this season of being single and you have decided to be happy and be a blessing, you can now focus on the fact that there are benefits to being single!

For example, you don't have to ask anyone for permission to go somewhere or do something that you want to do. If there is something you'd like to buy (and you have the money!), you don't have to ask anyone if it's okay with them. When you are married, you have to consider your spouse and what they might want. But as a single person, you are basically free to do what you want.

You are also free to devote more time to the things of God. The Bible says that people who aren't married can spend their time doing the Lord's work and thinking about pleasing Him, while married people have to think more about their earthly responsibilities and how to please their spouse.

But I would have you without carefulness. He that is unmarried careth for the things that belong to the Lord, how he may please the Lord:

But he that is married careth for the things that are of the world, how he may please his wife.

There is a difference also between a wife and a virgin. The unmarried woman careth for the things of the Lord, that she may be holy both in body and in spirit: but she that is married careth for the things of the world, how she may please her husband.

And this I speak for your own profit; not that I may cast a snare upon you, but for that which is comely, and that ye may attend upon the Lord without distraction.

1 Corinthians 7:32-35

As singles, we can be a big blessing to our church and to the kingdom of God. Remember, Jesus was single! And He did a lot for God, didn't He? God used Him in a great and mighty way.

Take advantage of the time you have as a single person, because later when you're married or have children, you won't have quite the same amount of time. Your time will be a little more occupied!

What you make happen for others, God can make happen for you.

Marry a Boaz Not a Bozo

One of my favorite stories in the Bible is about Ruth and Boaz, found in the book of Ruth. To give you some background, Ruth was a Moabite woman, which meant she grew up worshipping pagan idols. She didn't know God. But she married an Israelite who had come to live in the country of Moab.

Then her husband died, and so did her father-in-law. Ruth's mother-in-law, Naomi, was heartbroken and wanted to go back to her homeland of Israel. She told Ruth she could stay in Moab, but Ruth wouldn't hear of it. She loved Naomi and begged to be taken to Israel with her.

> *But Ruth replied, "Don't urge me to leave you or to turn back from you. Where you go I will go, and where you stay I will stay. Your people will be my people and your God my God.*
>
> *Where you die I will die, and there I will be buried. May the Lord deal with me, be it ever so severely, if anything but death separates you and me."*
>
> Ruth 1:16,17 NIV

So Ruth left her whole family and way of life to go with Naomi and take care of her. Back in Israel, Ruth went to work in the fields to support herself and Naomi, and she met Boaz, who was the owner of the fields. He was a honey with money! He fell in love with her and married her.

Because of Ruth's faithfulness to Naomi and because she turned to God, the Lord ended up rewarding her by giving her a new husband, a son, and a privileged position in the lineage of King David and even Jesus Christ Himself.

I want you to notice that Ruth wasn't seeking after a husband. She was laying down her life for someone else by serving a woman of God. She was putting the things of God first. So God made sure she got the desire of her heart.

What you make happen for others, God can make happen for you.

> *But seek ye first the kingdom of God, and his righteousness; and all these things shall be added unto you.*

> Matthew 6:33

Notice this Scripture says, "seek ye *first*," not third, fourth, or fifth! When you put God first by seeking Him (through daily prayer and Bible reading), He will see to it that you are rewarded.

> *...for he that cometh to God must believe that he is, and that he is a rewarder of them that diligently seek him.*

> Hebrews 11:6

The Greek word for *rewarder* means "wage payer."[2] In other words, it pays to serve God!

We need to seek God instead of seeking a mate. He will take care of the rest. The story of Ruth is a good reminder that when God rewards you, He does better than anything you could do for yourself. God has a Boaz waiting for you, so don't settle for Bozo!

3

PREPARATION TIME IS NEVER WASTED TIME

3

PREPARATION TIME IS NEVER WASTED TIME

While you're believing God to bring you the best, focus your attention on *becoming* the best *you* can be.

To do that, you'll need preparation time. Jesus took thirty years to prepare for a three-year ministry. Solomon took seven years to build the temple. Moses was in the house of Pharaoh and on the backside of the mountain for years before he stepped into God's plan to deliver Israel from Egyptian bondage. Any good marriage needs a good foundation. The bigger your dream is, the greater the foundation that has to be laid.

Take advantage of this time by preparing yourself for your future and your mate.

Maybe it seems as if it's taking a long time for the right person to come into your life. But why not take advantage of this time by preparing yourself for your future and your mate?

Don't Get in a Hurry

Don't let the devil make you feel anxious about getting married. You don't want to get in a hurry. People who rush into things many times just end up frustrated or hurt. It's a big mistake to rush into marriage because you are overeager, and you end up settling for second best.

Have you ever bought something in a hurry and settled for second best? For example, one time I found a pair of shoes that I absolutely adored. Only they didn't have them in my size. The shoe salesman came out from the back room with a pair that was a half-size smaller, assuring me not to worry because they would stretch. Have you been there? I tried the shoes on and they looked beautiful, but my feet were in pain! Guess what I did? I bought them anyway, because they looked good!

Well, the next week I preached in them, and I could hardly concentrate on my sermon because all I could think about was needing a healing in my feet! They hurt so badly!

We need to prepare and become like the person we're believing for.

I settled for second best. At least it was only a pair of shoes and not a husband! Don't settle for marrying someone who you know isn't the right one for you. In the end, you'll be glad you waited.

Prepare Yourself

Thus also faith by itself, if it does not have works, is dead.

James 2:17 NKJV

If you desire to be married and you are believing God to send you a mate, you must realize the importance of preparing yourself so that you're ready when he or she shows up. If you want your future mate to be getting prepared for you, then you should be getting prepared for that person! During this preparation time, keep trusting that God is working in both of you while you are waiting and that at the right time He will cause your paths to cross.

What's on Your List?

Most of the single people I meet have a list of things they're looking for in a mate. And that's good! But we need to be realistic about some of the things on our list, and most importantly, we need to look first at ourselves. Do we match the person we are looking for?

Let me give you an example. I knew one woman who had a really long list of things she wanted in a husband. He had to be a millionaire, and she wanted him to be in really good shape—she wanted a "Mr. Muscle." But the funny thing was, this lady herself was in debt up to her eyebrows, and she was 70 pounds overweight! That's probably never going to work!

We need to prepare and become like the person we're believing for. If you're ten pounds overweight, you can't say, "I don't want anyone who's even one pound overweight."

In other words, if you want someone who is toned and gorgeous, then *you* need to work at becoming more like that. If you want someone who is good with money, *you* need to become a person who is good with money. The simplest way to say it is: You need to become what you are looking for.

Practical Ways To Begin Preparing Yourself

Let's look at a few practical tips to prepare yourself for marriage.

The Spiritual Side of Preparation

Being strong spiritually is the foundation of your success in every area of life. This is the most important area in which we should be prepared. You can use this season of being single to study the Bible and get to know God better.

If you're believing to marry a great man or woman of faith and prayer, then that's what you need to become yourself. If you want to marry a person who walks in love, then become a person who walks in love.

1. Prepare yourself spiritually.

How do you become stronger spiritually? There are some basic keys that are vitally important to your spiritual growth. These are not hard things, but they are the foundation for a successful Christian life.

a) Prayer

Prayer is simply communicating with God. Talk things over with Him. Spending time in His presence will renew your strength (Isa. 40:31), bring you joy (fullness of joy, pleasures forever more), and just make your day a whole lot better.

(Ps. 16:11.) Never underestimate the power of prayer. Prayer changes things.

> ...*The earnest (heartfelt, continued) prayer of a righteous man makes tremendous power available—[dynamic in its working].*

> James 5:16 AMP

There is so much more to say about the subject of prayer, but that would be another whole book! There are many great books on prayer that you could read to enhance your knowledge on the subject. The important thing is that *you do it!*

b) Personal Bible Study

> *Study to shew thyself approved unto God, a workman that needeth not to be ashamed, rightly dividing the word of truth.*

> 2 Timothy 2:15

It's important that you spend time reading the Word of God. The Bible is God speaking to you. You can't live a successful Christian life without it.

When you read the Bible, you are feeding your spirit. Just like your natural man needs food to be strong and even exist, so must we receive spiritual strength by feeding on the Word. The book of Joshua says it this way:

> *This book of the law shall not depart out of thy mouth; but thou shalt meditate therein day and night, that thou mayest observe to do according to all that is written therein: for then thou shalt make thy way prosperous, and then thou shalt have good success.*

> Joshua 1:8

c) Regular Church Attendance

Let us not give up meeting together, as some are in the habit of doing, but let us encourage one another—and all the more as you see the Day approaching.

Hebrews 10:25 NIV

"The natural and the supernatural together make an explosive force for God."

It's so important for you to be a part of a local church. Just being in an atmosphere with other believers worshipping the Lord is your lifeline.

You need to find a good Bible-believing church that feeds your faith and helps you to keep growing. (If you need to find a good church in your area, I would be glad to help you. Just e-mail me on my Web site, www.katemcveigh.org.) If you are believing God for a Christian spouse, then he or she should be a committed churchgoer. And if you don't attend church, how are you going to meet that person?

d) Hearing the Word

My life was changed by constantly listening to teaching tapes. This is a great way to build yourself up. You can pop a tape in your car while you're driving to work.

So then faith cometh by hearing, and hearing by the word of God.

Romans 10:17

The Natural Side of Preparation

Once you have a handle on the spiritual part and you're getting things in place as far as seeking God, there are some other areas in the *natural* that also need to be prepared. Many times people overlook the importance of this side of things, saying, "God will take care of it." I like what one great man of God says: "The natural and the supernatural together make an explosive force for God."

We need to have the spiritual side of our lives in order, and we also need to have the natural side in order, too. We want to get ready and be the best we can be when the right man or woman comes along, right? The following are some natural areas to work on.

2. Prepare yourself physically.

One of the ways I started to prepare myself a few years ago was to lose some weight and get in better shape. If you don't want to marry someone who is really overweight, then you may need to do something about it yourself. It's important not only for you to look good, but to be healthy.

Let's admit it, what usually first draws you to a person is their appearance. Do you know the saying, "You can't judge a book by its cover"? The reason is that people do judge a book by its cover. Right or wrong, people are attracted to you (or not) by the way you look, at least at first.

Of course, you run the risk of having a great cover, with horrible insides! Even though looks matter, they definitely aren't everything. I remember meeting

Do the best you can with what you've got.

someone one time who was very handsome, and all the girls thought he was the best looking guy they ever saw. But once I got to know him better, he became very unattractive to me because of his personality.

What really matters is that you are attracted to someone. And many times once you get to know them better, what attracts you is their love for God, their sense of humor, or how thoughtful they are.

Let me just encourage you right now. God is not going to make you marry someone you are not attracted to. More than once I've had people frantically approach me because they had a fear that God wanted them to marry someone ugly.

One young man was afraid to pray about getting married because there was a girl in his church who really liked him. She was very unattractive to him, but he thought God would tell him that he had to marry her. Listen friend, God knows your desires, and He is not into punishing you by making you marry someone you don't want to marry. He's not that kind of God! He's good! He loves you, and He wants you to be happy!

a) Look Your Best

Another way to prepare yourself physically is to try and look your best at all times. Do the best you can with what you've got. It's amazing what the right clothes and make-up can do for a person. Anyone can look good by simply dressing right for their body type and making sure their clothes are clean and ironed. There are plenty of resources out there that can help you in this area.

When I was a teenager, I was very shy and lacked confidence. I was totally into sports and mainly wore sweat pants. Rarely did I make the effort to fix myself up, because I just wasn't all that interested. That's not a good way to impress anyone!

When I was in Bible school, I searched out some professional hair and make-up people who taught me how to improve my image. It can be hard humbling yourself and admitting that you need some assistance. But it's definitely worth it.

Years later, I remember sharing this experience with one of my employees who didn't fix her hair or wear make-up. She had so much potential of being very attractive, but she just didn't make the effort. As we talked about it, she told me she didn't care how she looked, but when it came right down to it, that wasn't true. The real root of the problem was that she had been hurt by men in her past and had a very poor self-image.

I encouraged her, prayed with her, and told her to get a hairy mole removed from her face. (I couldn't believe my boldness, because people who know me know that I'm not normally a confronter, but I cared about her so much that I had to tell her the truth.) She got set free that day because we got to the root of her problem, which was really rejection and low self-esteem. She learned how to apply make-up, began dressing very nice, got her mole removed, and took better care of herself. You would not believe the difference! Everyone around could tell that she had changed. Her level of confidence grew tremendously as a result. Her life was transformed as well as her looks.

b) Set Some Goals

I want to encourage you to try to look your best at all times. For one thing, you never know when you might meet Mr. or Ms. Right! Guys, you can shave, keep your hair neat, and stop dressing sloppy all the time. Ladies, you can fix your hair and make-up to the best of your ability. Ask the Lord to help teach you how you can improve in these areas.

The following is a sample of some goals you could set to prepare yourself physically. I will:

- Exercise or lose weight

- Take care of myself and try to be healthier

- Become more excellent in my appearance

When you get married, you're going to have to live with someone. So start preparing now to be someone whom a person would want to live with.

3. *Prepare yourself domestically.*

You know what else I've started to do to prepare for marriage? I'm learning to cook. Now I can push the buttons on a microwave pretty well! I have a friend who is a great cook, so I'm learning from her, and she's teaching me all the little secrets. It's something a wife should know how to do, at least a little bit. So I'm preparing myself.

When you get married, you're going to have to live with someone. So start preparing now to be someone whom a person would want to live with. If you're messy, start tidying up. If you're disorganized, try to get rid of some of the clutter in your life, and you will become more organized. It has been proven that people who keep things neat and orderly make room for success. I've heard that Donald Trump, a multimillionaire, hired a person full time to do nothing but keep things neat and orderly around him. He said that it causes him to think clearly and creates room for prosperity.

The following is a sample of some goals you could set to prepare yourself domestically. I will:

- Learn a new domestic skill
- Get rid of the clutter
- Become a more organized person
- Keep the house clean

4. Prepare yourself financially.

I know some people who are in such financial trouble that if God sent them a mate tomorrow, they couldn't afford to go on a honeymoon. They haven't been preparing financially; they've been irresponsible with their money. If you're believing God for a mate, you need to be getting ready by being diligent in your finances.

One time I dated a guy who was a good person and loved the Lord with all his heart. He was really nice, and he believed in healing, believed the Word, and believed all those faith things.

But he wouldn't get a real job. He worked part-time and never had any money, and that was good enough for him.

He wanted to marry me, but finally I had to ask him, "Listen, if I marry you, how would we pay for things like a honeymoon and a place to live?" Do you know what he said? "The Lord will provide." And I said, "Well, He's going to provide someone else for you! Good bye!"

Part of a woman's need is to feel secure and know that she will be taken care of by her husband. Second Thessalonians 3:10 says, "…if any would not work, neither should he eat." It's a biblical principle that a man should work.

All the way back in the book of Genesis, God gave His man Adam a job.

And the Lord God took the man, and put him into the garden of Eden to dress it and to keep it.

Genesis 2:15

Then notice what happens later in verses 21 and 22.

And the Lord God caused a deep sleep to fall upon Adam, and he slept: and he took one of his ribs, and closed up the flesh instead thereof;

And the rib, which the Lord God had taken from man, made he a woman, and brought her unto the man.

Genesis 2:21,22

God gave Adam the job first, and then He gave him a wife! According to the Bible, a man should get a job first then get a wife second.

If this man I was dating had really been trying to get his financial life in order, that would have been a different story. It's a heart issue. I'm not saying a person has to make a certain amount of money before I'll marry him, and you shouldn't either. It's not about the money; it's the principle. Are they willing to work and do something about getting their finances in order? Proverbs 10:4 says, "He becometh poor that dealeth with a slack hand: but the hand of the diligent maketh rich."

a) Saving and Getting Out of Debt

This guy who liked me was in his thirties. At this age they ought to have some money saved by now! As a matter of fact, you should regularly be putting money into a savings account, as well as thinking of your retirement fund. It's important to be knowledgeable in these areas, because it takes money to live! One of the major causes of divorce is money issues. You need to talk these things over with someone you may consider marrying.

If you want to marry someone who is debt free, then start working on being debt free yourself.

The same thing is true for women. They shouldn't be spending every penny they earn at the mall. It's okay to buy things for yourself if you can afford to. You should work at getting out of credit card debt right now if you need to. I have never paid interest on a credit card in my entire life. I went without in the beginning until I had the money to pay cash for things. And believe me, it has paid off.

I've always trained myself when I get paid to make saving the second thing I do after tithing and giving.

If you want to marry someone who is debt free, then start working on being debt free yourself. Maybe you've struggled in the area of finances. Now is the time to start learning how to handle them better, *before* you are married!

Get some help; start changing the way you do things. I read books on finances all the time that have helped me greatly. At a young age, I started preparing myself in some of these natural things. As I said earlier, I didn't wait for marriage to buy a house, so now I have some assets.

Do everything you can right now to get out of debt. No one wants to marry someone whose credit cards are charged up to the hilt or who is in trouble financially. Don't be discouraged, just start somewhere. You can do it!

b) God's Word on Finances

Here are some practical things the Lord has to say about prosperity:

Proverbs 10:4 tells us not to be lazy.

> *He becometh poor that dealeth with a slack hand: but the hand of the diligent maketh rich.*

Proverbs 24:30-34 give us clear instruction on laziness.

> *I went by the field of the slothful, and by the vineyard of the man void of understanding;*
>
> *And, lo, it was all grown over with thorns, and nettles had covered the face thereof, and the stone wall thereof was broken down.*

Then I saw, and considered it well: I looked upon it, and received instruction.

Yet a little sleep, a little slumber, a little folding of the hands to sleep:

So shall thy poverty come as one that travelleth; and thy want as an armed man.

That Scripture passage is talking about people who don't take care of things (like not mowing the lawn or not keeping the house up). It says that if all you do is sleep in and not work, poverty is inevitable.

Here are some benefits of being diligent in your finances. Notice this first Scripture says that the giver shall increase.

I think a man needs to open doors for a woman, and she needs to let him.

There is that scattereth, and yet increaseth; and there is that withholdeth more than is meet, but it tendeth to poverty.

The liberal soul shall be made fat: and he that watereth shall be watered also himself.

Proverbs 11:24,25

The blessing of the Lord, it maketh rich, and he addeth no sorrow with it.

Proverbs 10:22

Seest thou a man diligent in his business? he shall stand before kings; he shall not stand before mean men.

Proverbs 22:29

A good man leaveth an inheritance to his children's children: and the wealth of the sinner is laid up for the just.

Proverbs 13:22

The following is a sample of some goals you could set to prepare yourself domestically. I will:

- Tithe
- Put money in a savings account every month
- Put extra money toward reducing my credit card debt
- Stop buying things I don't have money to pay for
- Confess "I am debt free and money comes to me"

5. Prepare yourself socially.

Now, I'm kind of old-fashioned. I think a man needs to open doors for a woman, and she needs to let him. He needs to let her walk into restaurants ahead of him and perform other courteous behavior like that. Treat her like a lady. I'm just trying to give you some insight here. If you don't come from a background where you were taught these things, get an etiquette book and read it. Start preparing yourself!

I went to dinner with a guy one time, and I had some coaching from a pastor's wife before I went. She said, "Kate, don't you dare open the car door or the door to the restaurant you will be eating at." She made me promise that I would allow the gentleman to open the door for me. So I agreed.

When we pulled into the parking lot, he immediately got out of the car and headed straight to the door of the restaurant, and never looked back. I just sat in the car like she'd told me to do, waiting for him to open my door. It was so embarrassing! But I didn't move because I had promised I wouldn't open my own door.

Well, pretty soon he looked around and couldn't find me anywhere! Then he spotted me still sitting in the car, so he started to come all the way back. As he approached, I pretended I was digging for a mint in my purse so he wouldn't be embarrassed! He opened the door, apologizing.

He sort of messed up all night. He *did* open the restaurant door, but then when it was time to be seated at the table, he barged right in front of me and didn't allow me to go first the way he should have.

Some people are single for a season, and some people are single for a reason!

Do you know what? That guy didn't impress me very much. These things may sound a little picky to you, but they matter to me.

Now ladies, we have to know how to act right, too. I had one guy tell me after I preached on this subject at his church, "I'm glad you said that about holding doors open, because sometimes we don't know if we should. We don't know if we'll get clobbered for doing it!" We ladies have to brush up on this stuff too, so we'll let the gentlemen treat us right.

One thing that might help you, whether you're a man or a woman, is to get around people who know something about good manners. Hang out with them for a while and learn what they know. Prepare yourself to treat your future mate like you want to be treated. It's important.

I have a funny saying that goes like this: *Some people are single for a season, and some people are single for a reason.* We want to be sure that we're single just for a season and not for the wrong reason! When we do everything we can to prepare ourselves, then we're ready when our future mate shows up. You do your part, then keep trusting God to do His part.

Commit thy way unto the Lord; trust also in him; and he shall bring it to pass.

Psalm 37:5

The following is a sample of some goals you could set to prepare yourself socially. I will:

- Get a book on etiquette
- Spend time with someone who is more qualified than myself in respecting others
- Make a conscious effort to be mannerly, friendly, and thoughtful

4

"Honey Cometh!"
(How to Find
Mr. or Ms. Right)

4

"HONEY COMETH!"
(HOW TO FIND MR. OR MS. RIGHT)

You've probably heard the saying, "Money Cometh." Well, I invented a phrase called, "Honey Cometh!" kind of as a joke, but it really would be a good idea for you to believe your mate in. I especially like the phrase "Honey With Money," but anyway....

I really want to encourage you to get in faith concerning your future spouse. Start believing now that God will send you the right one. After you pray continue to make a faith confession, such as, "I believe I will marry the right person. God is having our paths cross at just the right time. I can hear from God; I will not miss it and marry the wrong one."

Romans 4:17 tells us to call "those things which be not as though they

> *Get in faith concerning your future spouse. Start believing now that God will send you the right one.*

were." So just start saying that your honey is on the way! "Honey cometh!"

What About Dating?

Right from the beginning, when I say the word "date" or "dating" I want you to understand what I mean. The word *dating* means a lot of different things to a lot of different people. When I refer to dating, I'm talking about something casual, getting to know each other, maybe going out to eat or something like that in a public place, even going out in a group. I'm not referring to a close or serious relationship.

> *You really need to spend a little bit of time with someone to see if you like them or not.*

I know a lot of Christian singles who are believing God for a mate, but they won't go on a date. They'll pray, "Lord, send me the right one," but if they're a guy, they won't ask a girl out, and if they're a girl and someone asks them out, they won't go! They're waiting for a big booming voice from heaven to say, "This is the one!" It usually doesn't happen that way.

I have heard about people who don't believe in ever going out on a date. They just supposedly hear God's voice and He says, "Marry that person." They never spend *any* time with each other until the wedding day, not even getting to know each other. Now, that's scary! To tell you the truth, I don't trust my ability to hear from God that much. What if I hear wrong?

What if I think God told me to marry this person, and then I find out that they're really not who they say they are?

A great way to hear from God is to follow after peace.

> *And let the peace (soul harmony which comes) from the Christ rule (act as umpire continually) in your hearts— [deciding and settling with finality all questions that arise in your minds,— in that peaceful state] to which as [members of Christ's] one body you were also called [to live]. And be thankful— (appreciative), [giving praise to God always].*
>
> Colossians 3:15 AMP

I liken it to a stoplight. Green means go. This is a peace on the inside. Red means stop. This could be a check or a knowing in your spirit that something's not right. Then there's the yellow light, which simply means to proceed with caution. (Although some people think it means to floor it and go faster!)

You really need to spend a little bit of time with someone to see if you like them or not. Sometimes just getting together can save you from spending hours of time in prayer! In many cases you can tell right away if you're interested or not.

Have you ever felt as if you've known who *isn't* the one for you? Does it seem as though you keep getting a "No, they're not the one" over and over again? The Bible gives an example of that in 1 Samuel 16. It tells how Samuel the priest went to the house of Jesse to find the next king of Israel. Once he arrived at the house, Samuel went down the line of all the brothers, ready to anoint the next king, but each time the Lord told him, "No, that's not the one."

I have felt that way sometimes when I've met people—"No, he's not the one!" But if you can know who is *not* the one, then you can know who *is* the one. Finally, Samuel had Jesse bring David in from watching over the flocks in the field, and as soon as Samuel saw him, God told Samuel, "That's the one!" And I believe God will help you and I to know the right one, too.

Guys, don't be afraid to ask a girl out just because you're afraid of being rejected. You know what? If you ask someone out and they say no, just ask someone else. Here's a little tip: be confident. Don't walk up to a girl hanging your head and mumbling, "You wouldn't want to go on a date with me, would you?" You're setting yourself up for failure asking her like that. Don't allow past hurts or the fear of being rejected stop you from taking a risk.

> *"Don't take this as rejection; take it as My protection."*

Rejection vs. Protection

Maybe you were involved in a relationship that didn't work out. Maybe you got "dumped," and you can't figure out why. It is driving you crazy trying to figure out why in the world they stopped liking you.

I had a similar experience once. I was feeling a little rejected because this person wasn't interested in me anymore. And I'll never forget the Lord speaking these words to me, "Kate, don't take this as rejection; take it as My protection."

In other words, the Lord was protecting me from being involved in the wrong relationship. He could see something that I could not see.

So if you've ever been dumped, don't let the devil lie to you and tell you there's something wrong with you. It could be that God was involved in removing that person out of your life for your own good. Really, I'm not all that surprised this happened to me because I often pray for God to remove any wrong influences or relationships from my life. This would be a great way for you to pray as well. It could save you years of turmoil and heartache.

You must find common ground in your beliefs, and make sure they're someone who is committed to the things of God like you are.

"Whom Should I Date?"

I don't believe in "missionary dating." What I mean is that the Word of God tells us we should not date someone who is not a Christian. Many times people go out with someone (and even go on to marry them) thinking that they can get them saved. Usually that ends up in heartache. The following Scripture is very clear.

> *Be ye not unequally yoked with unbelievers: for what fellowship hath righteousness with unrighteousness? and what communion hath light with darkness? And what concord hath Christ with Belial? or what part hath he that believeth with an infidel?*

> 2 Corinthians 6:14,15

You need to be looking for someone who believes like you do. You must find common ground in your beliefs, and make sure they're someone who is committed to the things of God like you are.

You can trust God to bring your mate to you.... You don't have to go out and beat every bush trying to find the right one for you.

For example, I won't even think about dating someone who doesn't believe in healing. Why? It's because that's how I'm going to be, and that's the direction that my life is going. If sickness attacks me, I want to be married to someone who can stand in the prayer of agreement with me for healing.

I know some singles may think that is narrowing the field too much, that there can't be that many people out there who believe like they do. But let me say this: God is able. No matter what age you are, God can bring you the desires of your heart. So don't be afraid, and set some guidelines for yourself.

How To Treat Each Other

Rebuke not an elder, but intreat him as a father; and the younger men as brethren;

The elder women as mothers; the younger as sisters, with all purity.

1 Timothy 5:1,2

The Scripture tells us that a man should treat a woman he's dating just like an older brother treats his younger sister. How would you treat your sister? You would honor her. The Bible is simply referring to treating one another with respect.

Looking for Love in All the Wrong Places

Have you ever felt so desperate that those "Christian Singles Dating Service" signs along the road start looking good to you? Or maybe you've looked in the newspaper and seen those personal ads that read, "Male seeking female." Don't be that desperate!

Remember, you can trust God to bring your mate to you. He said He would give you the desires of your heart. (Ps. 37:4.) Look to Him. You don't have to go out and beat every bush trying to find the right one for you. You probably wouldn't want what you find anyway! There are plenty of wrong places that people look for a mate, including those signs on the sides of buses or along the road.

I know Christians who hop from church to church trying to find their mate. Let me tell you, you don't have to go church hopping to find your spouse! Trust me, I go to hundreds of churches every year, and it doesn't work!

God knows where you are, and He can cause your path to cross with the one He's chosen for you. The best place for you to be is serving God faithfully in your local church, being about your Father's business.

Seek ye first the kingdom of God, and his righteousness; and all these things shall be added unto you.

Matthew 6:33

Keep your focus on Him and everything else will fall into line. You don't have to go looking.

You also don't want to hang out at singles' bars or worldly places like that. You won't find a man or woman of God in any of those places!

Know What You Want

There are some major things to consider before you get too interested in someone. For example, if you know that you want to get married and have children, and they don't, then the truth is, this relationship is just never going to work.

You can't jump into a marriage hoping the other person will change.

I remember talking with a close friend of mine. She met this guy at her church and they began to fall frantically in love, or so they thought. They made wedding plans, and as the day got closer, I remember asking my friend, "You have talked about important issues, right?" She told me that they did have a discussion about how many children they were going to have after they were married. She proceeded to tell me that she didn't want any kids, and he wanted three or four.

I immediately saw that as a red flag. I told her, "This probably isn't going to work," and she said, "The Lord will take care it."

Baloney! Listen, God's not going to take care of something like that; *you* need to take care of it.

This couple went ahead and got married anyway, and after one year, when the husband started wanting children, problems set in. And less than one year later they were divorced.

Was it God's fault that their marriage failed? No, you can't jump into a marriage hoping the other person will change. They weren't in agreement right from the start. You must be completely honest with yourself and each other about your dreams, goals, and future family plans.

It's important to know what matters to you, such as marrying someone who is much older or much younger than you are. There are some things to consider concerning this. I know in my case, I wouldn't want to marry someone twenty years older than me, even though someone else might not mind that. One of the reasons is that I want to have children, and he may have already had a family, and since he's been down that road, he doesn't want to go there again. It's important to really think these things though.

There are things that God knows about a person that you don't.

The Hidden Things Can Be Revealed

Let's say you have met someone whom you really like a lot, and you think that person may be the one for you. How can you be sure? One way is to pray that God reveals the hidden things to you.

> *For there is nothing hidden which will not be revealed, nor has anything been kept secret but that it should come to light.*
>
> Mark 4:22 NKJV

Maybe you're not quite sure about this person. They may even seem too good to be true. If there is something you need to know about them before you even consider them as marriage material, trust that God will show you anything that might need to be revealed.

Sometimes the person God has for you may be right under your nose. The Lord just needs to reveal that to you.

Hidden things can be bad or good things. There are things that God knows about a person that you don't. I have a friend who met a really nice guy who looked perfect on the outside. He was handsome, had a great car, wore great clothes, treated her like a queen, and went to church. She was totally swept off her feet. Everything was happening so fast that she became concerned that her judgment might have been too clouded to hear from God. So she told him they would have to take a week off from seeing each other so she could get in a place where she would be able to hear from the Lord.

She spent most of her spare time after work that week praying in the Spirit and claiming that the hidden things would be revealed, according to Mark 4:22. This man seemed perfect, almost too good to be true.

At the end of that week, as they talked on the phone, he began to reveal things to her in their conversation that he had never shared before, things she needed to know. This sent red flags flying, so she ended the relationship. Later, she discovered even more things about him. He was in trouble with the law and nearly bankrupt. She knew none of these things before she prayed. Thank God He protected her, and He will protect you too when you pray that hidden things be revealed.

An African Love Story

The hidden things being revealed aren't always the bad things. The Lord may start revealing to you their heart for Him. That happened to a missionary that I know. She met a guy, and at first, she thought he was kind of a geek. But as she prayed this Scripture and they talked more, she realized they had the same vision on their heart for the mission field, and he became more and more attractive and precious in her eyes. God revealed to her his good qualities and that he was a real man of God. They got married and have been serving God together on the mission field ever since.

The great part about this story is that she was a missionary in Africa for years and wondered how she would ever get married. How could she meet someone living way out in the bush? God sent this man to be a missionary all the way from America. They were both doing what God called them to do, and they each met the person of their dreams. If God can get someone all the way to Africa, He can get someone to you!

Sometimes the person God has for you may be right under your nose. The Lord just needs to reveal that to you.

5

Don't Settle
for
Second Best

5

DON'T SETTLE FOR SECOND BEST

If there's anything I want to do in this book, it's encourage you to *make sure it's God* when you're meeting a mate. Sometimes we can get so desperate to be married that we're willing to settle for second best, but don't do it!

Maybe you've met someone, and you like them a lot, but you say, "I don't know; they're good, but they're just not quite…." I like to say this: If they're "not quite," they're *not right!* God has something better for you if you'll trust Him and wait on His timing.

Don't get me wrong—there aren't any perfect people. You're going to have to walk in love and accept the imperfections

Don't get into a relationship with someone who can't flow with the vision that God has placed in your heart.

of whomever you end up marrying. (Because they'll have to accept yours!) Sometimes we know four or five different people and we want to take the best qualities from each one to make the best person for us. That's not going to happen! There are no perfect people in the world.

Sometimes you've got to "give up to go up."

But don't settle for something that you're not absolutely sure of. Don't say to yourself, "Well, they'll do." If all you can say is they'll do, then they're not for you! If you can do without, then throw it out. If you say "maybe," then it shouldn't be.

Don't Be Sidetracked From Your Vision

It's important that you find someone who believes in your dream, and you believe in theirs. Don't get into a relationship with someone who can't flow with the vision that God has placed in your heart. If God put a plan and a vision inside you, then He's well able to bring the right person along to hook up with it. And you can hook up with theirs.

One time a friend and I made an agreement with each other. We promised to be honest if we saw that one of us was about to make a mistake and marry the wrong person.

This friend of mine had graduated from Bible school and knew that God had called him to be a pastor. He needed a help-meet, someone who felt just as called in ministry as he did. He knew in his heart that he needed to marry someone who could help him fulfill his vision.

He was getting a little anxious and so got involved with a girl who had been married several times before and had lots of children. Besides that, she didn't feel called to the ministry. Everyone around him could see that he was making a big mistake— everyone except him that is. You've heard the saying, "Love is blind." Well, sometimes it can be! That's why you need to listen to people who care about you.

I remember having a serious talk with him, reminding him of what was in his heart for ministry, and the pact we had made to each other to be honest. The Lord began to deal with him about it. He realized he was about to make a big mistake, so the next day he called the whole thing off.

Do you know what happened? Exactly three months later, God brought the woman of his dreams along, and they eventually married. She is beautiful, loves God, and is totally dedicated to the ministry. Now they pastor a very successful church.

I believe many times the devil will send a counterfeit right before the real one comes along. I am so glad he listened to God, as they have a beautiful marriage.

This is a great example of how sometimes you've got to "give up to go up." My friend had to give up average to get extraordinary.

Many times the reason people date average, or settle for someone they're not really interested in, is because they're lonely.

Surround Yourself With Wise Counsel

I encourage you to be aware of the godly counsel God has placed in your life, such as your parents, pastor, close friends, and other committed Christians who care about you. The book of Proverbs has much to say about receiving advice from godly men and women.

> ...a man of understanding shall attain unto wise counsels.

Proverbs 1:5

> Where no counsel is, the people fall: but in the multitude of counselors there is safety.

Proverbs 11:14

> The way of a fool is right in his own eyes: but he that hearkeneth unto counsel is wise.

Proverbs 12:15

I like the one that says, "...in the multitude of counselors there is safety." Sometimes you can't see the forest for the trees. When you are too emotionally involved with someone, it becomes easy for you to overlook the obvious. It can be very obvious to others that this person may not be for you.

If all the people close to you think you are missing it with the current person you're dating, you should think twice about it and listen to their advice. Ask yourself this question: *Could they be right? What is their motive for telling me? Is it because they care about me?* They are most likely just trying to help you make sure you don't end up in a bad situation. And sometimes they can see things more clearly from outside the relationship, because their judgment isn't clouded by emotions. It pays to listen!

6

SEX AND
THE SINGLE
CHRISTIAN

6

SEX AND THE
SINGLE CHRISTIAN

Obviously, this is a big issue in the lives of single people. The world's idea of sex is totally different than God's idea.

Everywhere you look today, the world is telling you that it's okay to have sex outside of marriage. The idea is widely promoted that if you love someone, it's okay to have sex with them.

But the Bible doesn't say that! God says that sex is for marriage. The reason that God tells you to wait isn't because He wants to torture you and cause you to be unhappy. As a matter of fact, I have known many people whose lives are in turmoil because they didn't wait until they were married. It's not important what we believe about sex before marriage; it's what God believes. You and I must base our believing on God's Word.

A Word About Fornication

Flee fornication. Every sin that a man doeth is without the body; but he that committeth fornication sinneth against his own body.

1 Corinthians 6:18

This Scripture makes it clear that we are to wait until marriage to have sex. The Lord also gives you a tip in this verse by saying, "Flee…." To *flee* means "…to run away…"![1] In other words, get out of there! Go home! Take a cold shower!

Obviously, this issue must be important to God. He has reasons for telling you to wait.

I'm going to give you some things that will really help you to stay strong in this area, so keep reading.

In case you are not familiar with Bible terminology, the word *fornication* basically means sex outside marriage.[2] References to it appear over forty times in the Bible.[3] The word *adultery* means that you're already married, and you have sex with someone other than your spouse.[4]

God addresses this topic more than most others in the New Testament. For example, references to

- pride are mentioned three times[5]
- jealousy, five times[6]
- strife, twelve times[7]
- murder, twenty-two times[8]
- envy, seventeen times[9]
- drunk or drunkard, eighteen times[10]

- lying, fifteen times[11]
- stealing and thieves, thirty times[12]
- adultery, thirty-five times.[13]

But references to fornication appear thirty-nine times!

Obviously, this issue must be important to God. He has reasons for telling you to wait. For one thing, it messes you up emotionally, because sex is more than just a physical act. And just look at all the diseases that people can get from sex outside of marriage. Those are just a couple of reasons why God says it's important to wait.

What If You've Already Messed Up?

Maybe you have already fallen into temptation and had sex outside of marriage. The good news is, there is forgiveness for you.

> *If we confess our sins, He is faithful and just to forgive us our sins, and to cleanse us from all unrighteousness.*
>
> 1 John 1:9

This verse says that all you have to do is ask the Lord to forgive you, and He will. Don't allow the devil to make you feel guilty about it once you've repented. Get back up again, and don't look back.

If you're not there, you can't blow it!

There were even some people in the Bible who messed up big time in this area. We all know the story in 2 Samuel 11 about David and Bathsheba. David should have been at work, but instead he was home bored, watching something he had no business watching. (Does that sound familiar?) He saw Bathsheba taking a bath on her rooftop, and he wanted her, so he ended up sleeping with her. She was married, and the story keeps getting worse.

Guess what happened next? She got pregnant! Now David was all tripped out about it. But instead of telling the truth and repenting, he got a really dumb idea. As the leader of the army, he decided to send Bathsheba's husband, Uriah, right into the middle of the heaviest fighting. He basically sent him on a suicide mission, and he was killed.

So David had committed adultery and murder! But he eventually came to his senses and remembered how much he loved God. He repented for his mistakes, and God brought restoration to his life. After that, the Lord still referred to him as a man after His own heart. (Acts 13:22.)

God will do the same for you, no matter how bad you've blown it. God is a God of restoration! He can restore your life and get you back on track when you genuinely repent before Him as David did.

Set Boundaries for Yourself

The best way to stay strong and pure in the area of sex is to keep yourself away from places of temptation.

First of all, you can't mess up if you're not alone with someone. I call it "avoiding the scene of sin." Don't allow yourself to be in a position to fall. If you're alone with someone, the music is playing, the fire is burning, and the lights are dim, you know what usually happens next! You just can't put yourself in that position. Think about this: If you're not there, you can't blow it!

It's like when you're on a diet, it's dumb to hang out at the ice cream store, right? You might say, "Oh, I'm not eating, I'm just looking," but if you stay there long enough, you *know* what's going to happen—you're going to end up partaking! You're going to blow it! You're just asking for trouble by being there. The best way not to mess up is simply don't go there.

One thing I never do is let a man come over to my house alone. For one thing, it doesn't look good, and if I don't allow it, then there's no chance of stumbling. Notice that this next Scripture emphasizes the importance of setting the right example.

> *Abstain from all appearance of evil.*
>
> 1 Thessalonians 5:22

Think about it this way. If my neighbors ever saw someone leaving my house at two o'clock in the morning, that would not be a good witness. Even if nothing was happening and we were just visiting, they don't know that. We need to be a good Christian witness to those who don't know the Lord.

Set Boundaries for Married People

It's also not right for you to be hanging out with a married person of the opposite sex. For one thing, it gives people the wrong impression.

I have seen many marriages destroyed because of this. I noticed one day a girlfriend of mine who was married started hanging around a single guy. It first started out real innocently, because they were working together. Then they decided to start having lunches together, alone. Pretty soon he was giving her a lot of attention and compliments, although she still loved her husband and children.

At this point as a friend I tried to warn her, and even her husband warned her. But she refused to listen, saying we were all just being paranoid. I had a real serious talk with her about what was happening and the risk she was running of losing everything she had worked so hard for—her husband, her career, her children, and most importantly her walk with God. Sadly, that's what happened.

It's good to count the cost of falling into sin. I know of a man who was so serious about not falling into sexual sin that he made himself a list of everything it would cost him and the consequences of just a few moments of pleasure.

It's not you that you can't trust; it's your flesh that you can't trust.

He listed such things as losing the wife he loved so much and the hurt it would bring to her, not to mention the possibility of contracting a disease such as herpes or AIDS, and then the possibility of passing that on to his wife; losing his children and their respect and honor; his good name and reputation; his integrity; his career and livelihood; the hours and the money he had spent in college and everything he had worked so many years to achieve.

He told himself it wasn't worth the guilt and shame, or the barrier it would bring between him and God. Also, he knew it would disappoint so many people who respected him as a leader in the things of God, and it might cause them to stumble. He did not want to bring any reproach upon the kingdom of God.

Any time this man ever felt tempted, he would immediately get out his list and read it to himself. What a great idea! This man was really committed to integrity.

Most people never even think of the consequences; they just give way to the flesh. It would be a good idea to continually remind yourself of these things so you can keep yourself sharp and strong in the face of temptation.

You Can't Trust Your Flesh

Many times people get in compromising situations, saying, "Oh, I can handle it; I'm strong." Give me a break! Now, in your heart you want to do the right thing. You don't set out to fall into sin. But the real truth is, it's not *you* that you can't trust; it's your *flesh* that you can't trust.

How Jesus Overcame Temptation

Even Jesus Himself was faced with temptation. The devil came knocking at His door many times. It would help us to look at this whole passage of Scripture so that we could learn to handle temptation the way He did.

And Jesus being full of the Holy Ghost returned from Jordan, and was led by the Spirit into the wilderness,

Being forty days tempted of the devil. And in those days he did eat nothing: and when they were ended, he afterward hungered.

And the devil said to him, If thou be the Son of God, command this stone that it be made bread.

And Jesus answered him, saying, It is written, That man shall not live by bread alone, but by every word of God.

And the devil, taking him up into an high mountain, shewed unto him all the kingdoms of the world in a moment of time.

And the devil said unto him, All this power will I give thee, and the glory of them: for that is delivered unto me; and to whomsoever I will give it.

If thou therefore wilt worship me, all shall be thine.

And Jesus answered and said unto him, Get thee behind me, Satan: for it is written, Thou shalt worship the Lord thy God, and him only shalt thou serve.

And he brought him to Jerusalem, and set him on a pinnacle of the temple, and said unto him, If thou be the Son of God, cast thyself down from hence:

For it is written, He shall give his angels charge over thee, to keep thee:

And in their hands they shall bear thee up, lest at any time thou dash thy foot against a stone.

And Jesus answering said unto him, It is said, Thou shalt not tempt the Lord thy God.

And when the devil had ended all the temptation, he departed from him for a season.

Luke 4:1-13

How did Jesus handle temptation? What did He do about it? He rebuked it by saying, "It is written." So when temptation comes knocking at your door, resist it and rebuke it in the name of Jesus. Then run as fast as you can away from it! James 4:7 says, "…Resist the devil…and he will flee from you."

A Note to Women

One time my brother and I were having a discussion about temptation and how hard it is for men to stay pure when women dress so seductively. We were talking about how women "work it," so to speak.

My brother said that one time he and some friends were waiting in line at a restaurant, along with a girl he was taking out that evening. A woman walked by them whose clothes were so tight that she didn't leave much to the imagination. She walked by this whole group of people really "strutting her stuff," if you know what I mean.

> *As Christian singles, we don't have to dress or act like the world. We can still be "in" without compromising.*

Immediately every man's head turned toward her as she walked by. When she saw them staring, she stopped and looked at all the men with a disgusting look, as if to say, "What are you staring at?" So my brother said to her, "If you don't want us staring at your body, then don't put it on display!" That was a little bit bold, but he was right.

Sometimes women dress that way because they're insecure and they want attention. But they don't realize the message they're sending.

I also want women to dress modestly, with decency and propriety....

1 Timothy 2:9 NIV

As Christian singles, we don't have to dress or act like the world. We can still be "in" without compromising. The Scripture makes it clear that we should dress modestly. I don't mean that a Christian woman has to be a nerd or dress like her grandma, but she can still look beautiful without being seductive.

Sometimes women are sending the wrong message. It may not even be what they wear but how they're wearing it. Just be careful about what message you're sending. Don't make it even harder on men to resist temptation. Make it easier for them, and save yourself for the right one.

Let's look at several other ways to avoid temptation in the next chapter.

7

Five Keys
for Staying
Strong

7

FIVE KEYS FOR STAYING STRONG

The following are some tips that I believe will really help you stay strong and avoid temptation in the area of sex.

1. Pray.

One week without prayer makes one weak! Prayer keeps you spiritually strong to stand against temptation. These words came right from Jesus Himself:

> *Watch and pray, that ye enter not into temptation: the spirit indeed is willing, but the flesh is weak.*
>
> Matthew 26:41

One of the most powerful ways you can pray that will keep you strong is to pray in the Spirit.

One of the most powerful ways you can pray that will keep you strong is to pray in the Spirit. First Corinthians 14:4 says that praying in the Spirit edifies you.

Edify means to "build up,"[1] or you could say to charge up (like charging a battery). When you pray in the Spirit, you are building yourself up and charging your spiritual battery.

Likewise the Spirit also helpeth our infirmities....

Romans 8:26

> *You must allow your spirit man to be king. You rule over your body. Don't let your body rule you.*

Praying in the Spirit helps your infirmities. The word *infirmities* there actually means "...weaknesses...."[2] If you have a weakness in some area, then I encourage you to spend time praying in the Spirit, and the Holy Spirit will help you.

Many Scriptures tell us about the benefits of praying in the Spirit; here are a couple more.

He who speaks in a [strange] tongue edifies and improves himself....

1 Corinthians 14:4 AMP

For with stammering lips and another tongue will he speak to this people.

To whom he said, This is the rest wherewith ye may cause the weary to rest; and this is the refreshing.

Isaiah 28:11,12

Praying in the Spirit has helped me more than any other one thing.

2. Put your flesh under.

> But I (Paul) keep under my body, and bring it into subjection: lest that by any means, when I have preached to others, I myself should be a castaway.
>
> 1 Corinthians 9:27

Notice, Paul says that *he* kept his body under. So who does the keeping? We do! How do we do this? One of the most important ways is to keep your mind on the right thing.

You must allow your spirit man to be king. You rule over your body. Don't let your body rule you.

3. Avoid the scene of sin.

Remember, if you are not in a position to be tempted, you cannot fall. Avoid anything that you know would cause you to stumble, such as being in the wrong place at the wrong time with the wrong person!

4. Watch what you watch.

I believe that men are even more susceptible in this area because they are so visually oriented. No wonder it's so hard for men today—temptation is everywhere. A surprising number of women, especially in the world, don't know how to dress modestly. On many street corners, there are billboards filled with suggestive advertising that feature half-dressed women. Some of these things you can't avoid seeing, but you can avoid staring at them.

Be careful what you look at. Don't allow the devil to lure you into tempting Internet sites or wrong movies. Some people innocently glance at these things, and then it gets a bigger hold on them until finally they yield themselves to such a degree that it becomes a stronghold. Discipline yourself to focus on the right things.

5. *Spend time in the Word.*

You have to feed your spirit daily to keep yourself strong. Just as you feed your natural body to keep it strong, so must you feed your spirit man. If you go for days without eating or drinking water, your body will get weak and become dehydrated. One reason why people have a hard time resisting temptation is that they are spiritually weak and dehydrated.

> *No one ever got into sexual sin without thinking about it first.*

If you faint in the day of adversity, your strength is small.

Proverbs 24:10 AMP

How does someone's strength become small? It happens by not feeding it the Word. Feed your spirit the Word of God and you'll be strong.

Think About What You're Thinking About

The battlefield for all Christians is in their mind, and that's especially true for singles. It's true in every realm of our life, but especially in keeping ourselves pure in this realm of sex.

But I say to you, that everyone who looks on a woman to lust for her has committed adultery with her already in his heart.

Matthew 5:28 NASB

The same is true for women looking at men. This Scripture is stressing the importance of a pure thought life. You have to keep your thoughts in check. Think about what you're thinking about! Don't just allow yourself to think about whatever feels good. The mind is a powerful thing, and no one ever got into sexual sin without thinking about it first. Are your thoughts glorifying God? If not, ask Him for help.

Just as God created the world with words, you and I can create our world around us by the words of our mouth.

Casting down imaginations, and every high thing that exalteth itself against the knowledge of God, and bringing into captivity every thought to the obedience of Christ.

2 Corinthians 10:5

This Scripture says that we are to cast down imaginations, but many times we're letting those imaginations cast us down instead! It also says to take every thought captive. Don't let thoughts take you captive.

When you fly overseas, after landing, you must go through customs. Often they scan through your luggage to make sure you don't bring anything into their country that doesn't belong there. It would be a good idea if we set up our own "spiritual customs agency" in our mind. When thoughts come to us, we must scan those thoughts. If they are not pure thoughts, then we don't let them through into our "country," so to speak.

Just because you have a wrong thought doesn't mean that you have sinned. It's when you meditate on that thought and act upon it that you miss it. Jesus talked many times in the Gospels about taking no thought. You may have a thought of sexual sin, but *just don't take it* by acting on it or meditating on it.

I like what one minister I know says, "You can't keep the birds from flying over your head, but you can keep them from making a nest in your hair."

The best way to counteract a wrong thought is not just with a thought. In other words, you don't fight a thought with another thought. You fight thoughts with words. Your words are more powerful than your thoughts. When you are speaking faith-filled words, those wrong thoughts can't remain.

Just try to count to ten inside your head, and at the same time, try to say your name out loud. What happens? Your words interrupt your thoughts, and you stop counting. When Satan tempted Jesus, the way He resisted him was with words. He said, "It is written." Even when God created the world in the book of Genesis, He didn't just *think*, "Let there be light," even though He could have (Gen. 1:3). Rather, He chose to *say*, "Let there be light." Just as God created the world with words, you and I can create our world around us by the words of our mouth. We can create a world of health, healing, and right thinking. Your words will overpower wrong thinking.

The Bible tells us what we should be thinking about.

> ...*whatsoever things are true, whatsoever things are honest, whatsoever things are just, whatsoever things are pure, whatsoever things are lovely, whatsoever things are of good report; if there be any virtue, and if there be any praise, think on these things.*
>
> Philippians 4:8

You can win the battle of the mind and remain sexually pure.

8

ARE YOU LONESOME TONIGHT?

8

ARE YOU LONESOME TONIGHT?

Have you ever started feeling so sorry for yourself that you played Elvis Presley's song, "Are You Lonesome Tonight?"[1] and spent the rest of the evening crying?

As a single person, it's important for you to know that you can be alone without being lonely. I travel all the time and stay in hotels by myself, but you know what? I enjoy it. I enjoy being by myself and spending time with God, and you can too. He is always there for you. The Bible says that when we draw near to Him, He draws near to us. (James 4:8 NKJV.)

I also want you to remember that you're never really alone. The Bible is full of evidence that shows you have the Greater One, the Holy Spirit, living right on the inside of you, and He's with you wherever you go! Matthew 28:20 says,

You can be alone without being lonely.

"...and lo, I am with you alway, even unto the end of the world...." That is good news! Jesus said in Hebrews 13:5, "...I will never leave thee nor forsake thee." That means everywhere you go, He is with you.

Maybe you're reading this book today and you've been divorced or widowed, or maybe you've never been married, but you're just lonely. I want you to know that the Holy Spirit wants to comfort you. Your life isn't over! God is a God of second, third, and fourth chances.

> But the path of the righteous is like the light of dawn, that shines brighter and brighter until the full day.
>
> Proverbs 4:18 NASB

Notice that doesn't say your path is getting dimmer and dimmer. Your future is bright!

God is your Helper and your Comforter in times when you don't know what to do. In John 14:16-18, Jesus said, "And I will pray the Father, and he shall give you another Comforter, that he may abide with you for ever; Even the Spirit of truth...for he dwelleth with you, and shall be in you. I will not leave you comfortless...." You can lean on Him when you need comfort.

"God Is Helping Me!"

I have a friend whose husband recently went home to be with the Lord. She is about sixty-five years old and a wonderful saint of God, and of course, it was so hard on her when her husband died. She missed all the things that they did together, like eating and fixing things together around the house.

But one day shortly after his death I called her on the phone to ask how she was. I told her, "I know you miss your husband tremendously. But God cares so much about you that He is going to be an even greater Husband to you, because you need Him." And she said, "You know what? I'm beginning to see that. God is helping me."

> *Find people who are of like, precious faith with whom you can fellowship.*

She really pressed into believing for the comfort of the Holy Spirit. And she said, "Every time I have a need arise in my life, the Lord sends someone to meet it. I'm experiencing the supernatural comfort of the Holy Spirit. I almost feel guilty because God is helping me so much!"

Thank God for the Holy Ghost! You can count on Him!

"Do not be afraid; you will not suffer shame. Do not fear disgrace; you will not be humiliated. You will forget the shame of your youth and remember no more the reproach of your widowhood.

For your Maker is your husband—the Lord Almighty is his name...."

Isaiah 54:4,5 NIV

If you are a single woman, God is your Husband! Whether you are male or female, divorced, widowed, or never been married, you might be hurting today because of loneliness. I want to encourage you to bathe your spirit in these Scriptures.

Then as much as you can, focus on what is good in your life, and put your faith in God.

Good Friends Are Important

Whenever I start to feel lonely or discouraged over being single, I call somebody. I go out and do something, or I reach out to someone. It's so important to have good friends! I try to surround myself with people who will encourage me.

I have one set of friends, a married couple, who are such good friends that I can just call them up anytime and invite myself over. Sometimes I spend the night at their house. They have always told me that if I'm ever feeling a little down, I can just call them up and come over.

Find people who are of like, precious faith with whom you can fellowship. If there's nobody like that in your life, ask God to send you someone. Say, "Lord, send those people my way."

A man that hath friends must shew himself friendly....

Proverbs 18:24

According to the Bible, in order to have friends, you have to *be friendly*. Sometimes that means you have to go out of your way, outside of your comfort zone, and be friendly to someone else. You know, someone out there might need *you* as a friend.

So do your best to not focus all your attention on yourself. Take the first step. Be courageous. Make the extra effort, even if it's hard for you to walk up and introduce yourself to someone. Don't just sit around and wait for the phone to ring; pick it up and call someone and go do something. It will make all the difference in your life.

9

TEN WRONG REASONS FOR GETTING MARRIED

9

TEN WRONG REASONS FOR GETTING MARRIED

I think you can tell by now that there are plenty of wrong reasons for marrying someone. When we get married, it's supposed to be for the rest of our life, so we want to really make sure we can spend the rest of our life with this person.

It's important that we marry someone for the right reasons and not the wrong reasons.

The following are some wrong reasons for getting married.

1. *Pressure from family or friends.*

There may be a certain person whom your family or your friends really like. They may think you've waited long enough to get married, so you'd better grab this one while you can. But you're the one who's marrying this person; they're not the ones who have to live with them day in and day out for the rest of their lives!

I have a friend who felt pressure to marry someone because my friend's parents really liked the person. So they got married, and my friend was miserable for a long time. They trusted God to heal their marriage and make it special, and now they are finally happy, but they went through a battle that God never intended for them to have to fight.

Don't get me wrong. I think your parents' advice and the advice of people close to you is important. But ultimately *you* are the one making a lifelong commitment. It's important not to give in to pressure from other people, but to marry the one God has placed in your life and you know is right for you.

2. *Your biological clock is ticking.*

Tick tock, tick tock. Have you ever been sleeping by a clock and listening to it ticking, thinking, *That's me! Time is running out—my biological clock is ticking?*

This is a very real feeling, especially for women. You may want to get married and have a family, and it feels as though time is short. Just remember, God knows the desires of your heart. He knows if you want children, and He can make a way for you, even when it seems as if there is no way. Marrying the wrong person just because you feel as though there's no more time left can still lead to a miserable future.

Just because your answer is delayed doesn't mean it's been denied.

I have a friend who waited a long time to get married, and she desperately wanted a family. She got married in her late thirties, and do you know what God did for her? He gave her twins! That's the blessing of God; He gave her double. (Isa. 61:7.)

You too can have double for your trouble. God always makes it worth your wait! Just because your answer is delayed doesn't mean it's been denied. Just because you've waited a long time doesn't mean you're not going to get it. There are times when people experience a "divine delay." In other words, there are still some things the Lord may want you to receive where you are right now, before you move on to another season.

In my own life, there are many things I have done for the Lord that I really don't believe I could have done in the same way had I been married with children. We have to learn to trust our heavenly Father and His love for us. He knows what we need and when we need it. Father knows best! God loves you, and He will give you the desires of your heart.

3.   You're lonely.

Although we have already talked about this, just let me say again that you don't want to marry someone just to keep from being alone. There are a lot worse things than being single, and plenty of married people are desperately lonely. Marrying the wrong person won't solve the problem of loneliness; only God can do that.

Being alone doesn't mean you have to be lonely. Don't be so desperate that you just marry anybody to keep from being alone.

4. *You're tired of being a third wheel.*

Do you ever feel as if the whole world is a couple except you? Or do you ever wonder if couples just invite you along somewhere because they feel sorry for you?

I have a friend who hates to go to a restaurant with couples because there always seems to be an even number of chairs at the table, and no one can figure out whom she should sit next to. Or she feels awkward that someone else's husband is always having to open the door for her or pull out her chair. But you don't get married just because you want to be a couple.

5. *Someone loves you and/or needs you.*

I got to know a Christian man one time who was head over heels in love with me, and I didn't feel the same way about him. I was flattered by how much he loved me, and pretty soon I was in love with the fact that he loved me. But it wouldn't have been fair to him to marry him knowing that I didn't love him the same way he loved me, even though he was a really nice guy.

Looks will fade and bodies will change, so what's important is what's on the inside of someone.

You also don't want to marry someone just because they need your help. Some of us are such givers that we want to help people. I've known of people getting married just because one of them told the other one, "I can't live without you." That's a wrong reason to get married!

6. *Based on their looks alone.*

It's important to be physically attracted to the person you marry, but on the other hand, you can't marry someone based on looks alone. Looks will fade and bodies will change, so what's important is what's on the inside of someone.

Have you heard the saying, "The lights are on but nobody's home"? I have met several very attractive guys and if I were marrying them based on looks, I would be married now! But I found out they didn't have much integrity, character, or even common sense.

Sometimes women can use their looks to get what they want, but that's wrong, too. A woman may be beautiful and attractive and play the field with different men. That may be the kind of woman some guys like to date, but they don't usually want to marry them. A woman like that might not be a good mother to their children or be the godly woman that they really are searching for deep inside.

Money is important, but it's not everything!

7. *You think no one else may want you.*

Don't settle for the wrong person just because you think there's no one else out there for you. If you want to be married, God has the right one for you! Don't marry the first person who comes along just because you're desperate.

Often times there may be a counterfeit right before the real thing. Maybe you have found someone who really loves you, but you don't care that much for them. Don't marry them just because you think they're your last chance, and no one else may want you. God has someone special waiting in the wings just for you.

8. *Money only.*

Money is important, and it takes money to live, but it shouldn't be your only reason for getting married. You can marry someone rich and be miserable if they're not the right one for you.

I had two opportunities to do that. I met one guy whose dad was a billionaire, and if I were going to marry someone just for money, I would have married him. He was a Christian, but there were things in his life that disqualified him as a good husband.

There was another guy who was very wealthy and he liked me, but I have to be honest—he had a really big nose, and I just couldn't live with it. He had over $12 million in savings alone, and all my friends teased me saying, "Kate—$12 million! You could fix his nose!"

But even though I would have had a lot of money, I don't think I would have been happy, because there were some other issues that just didn't work.

Money is important, but it's not everything! I know someone who said she's going to marry for money only, and she's still single. She dated some really famous people, but I think they could tell she just wanted to marry someone with money. No one wants to marry someone like that!

9. *You need help.*

We could be talking here about help to raise your children, help around the house, help in your business, or any number of things. And a spouse *should* help you with all those things, but that shouldn't be the *only* reason you marry someone.

10. *You want to have sex.*

This subject was pretty well addressed in a previous chapter, but it still needs to be on this list. Some people rush ahead and get married just so they can have sex, but then they regret it later. Maybe their heart was right, wanting to get married before they have sex, but they move too quickly before they really get to know the person.

You need to make sure that you don't rush into marriage just to meet certain physical needs. Ask God to help you and give you strength to wait for the right one.

10

BEFORE
YOU SAY,
"I DO"

10

BEFORE YOU SAY, "I DO"

Once you've found the person you believe God wants you to marry, there are some important things that the two of you need to consider, talk about, and agree upon together before you say "I do." There are also certain things you need to understand about the opposite sex and their needs. That's what I want to cover in this chapter.

The Importance of Counseling

First of all, let me say that it's so important for you to go to premarital counseling before you get married. Your pastor could probably recommend some good reading material to you along these lines as well.

Knowledge is power. The more you learn ahead of time the better your marriage can be. Much of what we will

The more you learn ahead of time the better your marriage can be.

You're not going to agree on every little tiny thing, but the main issues are important.

discuss here is usually brought out in even more detail in your premarital counseling sessions. It is vitally important that you talk about these things and take them very seriously. The strength of your marriage depends on it.

Here are the top five most important things that you need to discuss before marriage. These are almost always the top five leading issues on why people get divorced.

1) Religion
2) Money
3) Sex
4) Children
5) Career/work

Religion

When I say the word "religion," I mean your spiritual beliefs. It is important that your marriage is based on a solid foundation. If your potential mate is not on the same wavelength with you spiritually, it can be a problem. As we've already discussed, the Bible makes it very clear to make sure you marry a Christian.

Be ye not unequally yoked together with unbelievers: for what fellowship hath righteousness with unrighteousness? and what communion hath light with darkness?

2 Corinthians 6:14

These are the issues that are important to me: that I marry someone who believes like I do where healing, the baptism of the Holy Spirit, and other doctrinal issues are concerned. I want to know that if I have a problem, I can pray with my spouse and agree together in faith for an answer. But if they don't believe the same way that I do, there will be a problem.

Now, I know you're not going to agree on every little tiny thing, but the main issues are important.

Can two walk together, except they be agreed?

Amos 3:3

Doctrinal beliefs are very important, especially when it comes to raising your children. One person I know settled for and married a nonbeliever, and every night when she prays with her children, they ask her, "Why doesn't Daddy pray with us?" It makes her life very hard.

Money

Let's face it, it takes money to live, and you have to find out where you are in that area. You may have been raised in a fairly well-to-do home and are used to a certain lifestyle. You have to be honest about what lifestyle you expect to have when you're married.

Discuss your financial goals, to make sure you're on the same page financially.

Maybe your potential spouse didn't come from the same background, or they don't care about the same things you care about. Maybe they're not inspired to work hard, and you can't live like that. All of those things are important to talk about.

Find out about the other person's spending habits and their saving habits. I know couples who are on the brink of divorce because one of them is spending all the money faster than it comes in. This creates a lot of stress. Find out before the wedding if they're in debt. You need to know ahead of time what you'll be facing.

I know a pastor who goes as far as having couples bring in their bank statements, W-2's, debts, and bills when they come for premarital counseling. That way everything is out in the open. At first that sounded a little extreme to me, but then I heard that by doing it, some people found out things that really needed to be addressed before it was too late. It was an eye-opening experience for many of them.

Talk together about your plans for tithing and giving. It would be very hard if you're a committed tither and then find out that they're not. Discuss your financial goals to make sure you're on the same page financially.

Don't forget, one of the top reasons that couples get divorced is because of money problems.

Sex

You don't really want to get into intimate details of sex until you're pretty sure that this is the one God has for you.

I'm not going to go into much detail here, but be sure that you talk about it. Couples have to be in agreement and know how the other one thinks and believes about this issue.

Children

It's important that you be in agreement whether or not you want to have children and how many you want. Don't have the thought, *Maybe they'll change their mind and want to have kids later.* Make sure you know first. I wrote earlier about the couple whose marriage didn't last because they didn't take this issue seriously enough and they ignored it, hoping it would change later. And they ended up in divorce court.

> *You shouldn't marry someone who isn't willing to back your dream.*

Another very important thing to consider is what you both believe about raising children. How to discipline your children and what you believe along these lines is a huge issue in many families. So it's important to talk about it beforehand.

Career

This issue is something to consider. I know for example in my own life, I have a call from God to preach the Gospel around the world. This sometimes can be a little challenging when it comes to thinking about whom I'm going to marry because I have a strong ministry. It can be intimidating in a way because it can seem backwards. It's often a man who has the stronger calling.

In my case it would be hard to marry someone else who has a strong preaching ministry. I would rather marry someone who is willing to help me with what God has called me to do. Some people used to try to make me feel guilty for being honest in this area, but I don't apologize for it anymore. In the beginning of my ministry, when no one knew who I was, people used to try to make me feel bad for not giving up what I'm doing to go help someone do something else (like pastor a church). But I knew I had a different vision in my heart—I saw myself traveling around the world, and I knew I wouldn't be happy unless I did it.

Of course, now people can see that I was following the Lord because what I had in my heart is coming to pass. Only you and God know what's in your heart. You have to be sure you discuss this with your potential mate.

Each of you has to find out what the other expects in this area. If you're a woman, will your husband expect you to quit your career to get married? Or is that what you want? Be sure you're in agreement.

What's in your heart for the future? Your visions basically need to be flowing in the same direction. For example, if a man feels called to the ministry, he must marry someone who is willing to go wherever the Lord sends him. If you're called to Africa, you have to know that your mate is willing to set aside their own desires and go with you.

One of my staff members is married to a man in medical school. They knew going into the marriage that they wouldn't see much of each other for the first few years because of the intense training that is required to be a doctor. They both know it's an investment right now, but it will pay off in the long run.

You shouldn't marry someone who isn't willing to back your dream, or you have to be honest if you can live without your dream. If they don't fit with your vision, you need to find that out *before* you are married.

Marriage Is About Walking in Love

Love endures long and is patient and kind; love never is envious nor boils over with jealousy, is not boastful or vainglorious, does not display itself haughtily.

It is not conceited (arrogant and inflated with pride); it is not rude (unmannerly) and does not act unbecomingly. Love (God's love in us) does not insist on its own rights or its own way, for it is not self-seeking; it is not touchy or fretful or resentful; it takes no account of the evil done to it [it pays no attention to a suffered wrong].

It does not rejoice at injustice and unrighteousness, but rejoices when right and truth prevail.

Love bears up under anything and everything that comes, is ever ready to believe the best of every person, its hopes are fadeless under all circumstances, and it endures everything [without weakening].

Love never fails [never fades out or becomes obsolete or comes to an end]....

1 Corinthians 13:4-8 AMP

Walking in love means putting the other person and their needs before your own. I heard one minister say, "What would marriage be like if couples were always trying to outdo one another in love? It would be heaven on earth."

Imagine how sweet a marriage could be if each party went into it with a determination to meet the needs of their spouse. (Instead of only thinking about their own needs!)

If there is a disagreement or something you do need to let your spouse know about, don't embarrass them in public by correcting them.

When I was a teenager, I stayed in the home of one pastor and his wife for several weeks and got to experience first hand an example of a beautiful marriage. Every morning the pastor would bring his wife a cup of coffee in bed. He was always opening the car door for her and treated her like a queen. She, on the other hand, was always trying to outdo him in love by making him his favorite meal and speaking edifying words over him to build him up.

They also had a rule that they would never yell at each other in their home, and you could really sense the peace of God as a result. They came from "The Loud Family" where everybody screamed to get their point across. Did you come from "The Loud Family" too?

They made the decision that if their home would be different, they would have to work at it. One way they worked at it was if someone had a phone call and the person was in another room, instead of screaming, "Telephone!" they would put the phone down, walk all the way to the other end of the house, and quietly say, "The phone's for you." As a result, there was peace in their household.

I also noticed that she would never correct her husband in front of people, even in small things. For example, if he said something that wasn't completely accurate, like "There were 100 people at church," but there were only 90, she didn't correct him.

Have you ever seen people arguing back and forth over something trivial like that? One will say, "No, there were 90!" and the other will say, "No, there were 100!" and before you know it, they're arguing right in front of you. How embarrassing!

She taught me that if there is a disagreement or something that you do need to let your spouse know about, don't embarrass them in public by correcting them. Wait until you are alone, in private, and then you can come and say, "Honey, you might need to know this...."

They also made a decision that the word "divorce" would never be mentioned or even be considered as an option in their marriage. Even if they were mad or joking and didn't mean it, they would never allow themselves to say the words, "I want a divorce."

I learned so much from watching their example of walking in love towards each other. My parents are also a great example. They have a beautiful marriage after more than 45 years.

A man needs to know that his wife honors and respects him.

What we must realize is that love is a commitment and a decision, not a feeling. Have you ever heard people say, "I just don't love him (or her) anymore; I want a divorce"? That's the world's cop out. Love is a commitment in good times and bad. Remember in the marriage vow "for better or for worse"? That's a commitment.[1] As you walk in love, putting the other person first, you'll reap a harvest of love yourself because *love never fails.*

What Men Need, What Women Need

I thought it would be a good idea here to list five important needs of men and women. Before you say "I do," these are basic ingredients needed to have a happy, successful marriage. These are not the only five needs that men and women have, and they're not in any particular order, but they will be helpful to you. There are other great resources on these that go into more detail, but here are some basics.

What Men Need

1) Honor

A man needs to know that his wife honors and respects him. Ephesians 5:33 in *The Amplified Bible* says it like this, "…let the wife see that she respects and reverences her husband [that she notices him, regards him, honors him, prefers him, venerates, and esteems him; and that she defers to him, praises him, and loves and admires him exceedingly]".

First Peter 3:2 AMP tells wives, "[…you are to feel for him all that reverence includes: to respect, defer to, revere him—to honor, esteem, appreciate, prize, and, in the human sense, to adore him, that is, to admire, praise, be devoted to, deeply love, and enjoy your husband]."

2) Sex

It's true that men usually have a stronger desire than women do in this area. But a smart woman understands that a healthy sexual relationship means a lot to her husband, and this is an important key to his happiness. I'll say it again: These are things that you must discuss before you get married.

It means a lot to a man when his wife cares about what he cares about.

3) Loyalty and honesty

A man needs to know that he can trust his wife and that her heart is toward him alone. A real man of God desires a Proverbs 31 kind of woman—a woman of character and dignity. He is looking for someone who would be faithful to him as well as being a good mother to their children.

4) Domestic support

While this is important to both men and women, a man greatly appreciates as peaceful a home environment as possible. It is built into his nature to go out and work hard, then come home to a loving, supportive wife. In today's world many women have to work too, so this doesn't necessarily mean that every man is expecting a hot meal on the table and slippers waiting by his chair as his wife jumps to meet his every need. But it *does* mean that he wants to know his wife is supporting him and that they are working together to have a loving, nurturing home life.

5) Recreation

While men like to do certain "guy" activities on their own or with other male friends, it's very important to them to have at least one or two "playtime" activities that their spouse enjoys doing with them. It means a lot to a man when his wife cares about what he cares about.

I heard one woman who wasn't very athletic growing up say that she decided to take up golf just so she'd have something in common with her husband. She knew it was important to him that she do something recreational with him. Now they spend time golfing together, and they're closer than ever.

Some pastors whom I'm very close with were sharing with me how important this issue is to a man. One of them told me that his wife even went so far as to take up hunting and has gone on several hunting trips with her husband. That's a smart woman!

Women have a need to feel safe and protected.

What Women Need

1) Love and affection

A woman needs to feel loved and cherished by her husband. She is

BEFORE YOU SAY, "I DO"

happiest when she hears and sees his affection for her. Sometimes men feel that saying, "I love you" once is enough and that she should just know it from then on. But women need more than that because they are very emotional beings. They have a need for tender, genuine affection on a regular basis. That's why women like flowers, mushy cards, and they melt when a man whispers sweet nothings in their ear.

2) Communication/Conversation

It's a pretty well-known fact that women talk more than men. I've heard experts say that women have twice as many words to get out in a day than men do! I've also heard it said that the way women get rid of their problems is to talk them out. A woman needs to talk about things and have someone she loves *listen to her and understand what she's going through.* She needs to know they care. A common complaint of unhappy wives is, "We just don't talk to each other" or "He never listens to me." Have you ever noticed that women like details, whereas most men just give you the highlights? A wise husband knows that investing time in talking and listening to his wife will meet her needs and make their marriage happier.

3) Security

Women have a great need for stability and security, especially in the financial realm. They need to know that they will be taken care of financially. Women have a need to feel protected and safe. It's a big deal to them, and it might make men wonder how much they have to make before a woman will marry them.

It's not so much the amount as it is knowing that their husband is willing to work and take care of things. That makes a woman feel safe and secure.

4) Trust

Much the same as a man, a woman needs to know she can trust her husband. She needs to trust his ability to hear from God and be faithful to His Word. Where there is no trust there is no respect. A woman needs to know by the actions of a man that he is trustworthy. Trust is the foundation for a healthy relationship.

5) Family commitment

It is important to a woman for her husband to be "family minded." She needs to know that he will be committed to her and their children. She needs reassurance that she will come before his friends and that she and their children will come first. To be committed to family and each other is really being committed to God and His Word.

It means a lot to know a husband is committed to work together to attain their goals and build a family life and the right foundation.

In Conclusion

Remember, God has a great plan for your life no matter where you've been or what you're going through now. As you delight yourself in Him, He is bringing you the desires of your heart!

I want to pray for you:

As I pray for you, dear friend, I believe that even though you are single, you are never alone because God is with you. He has a great plan for your life, and your steps are ordered by Him. *Father, give my friend comfort and the peace that passes all understanding. Strengthen and encourage them in their walk with You.*

I believe that God is filling any void on the inside of you. I pray for supernatural, divine relationships and Holy Ghost connections to come your way and that even now, God is preparing you for what He has in store for you. If you desire to be married, I believe God is bringing your future mate across your path. I declare that you will marry the right person! God is big enough to give you the desires of your heart.

Father, thank You for giving my precious friend everything they need to be an uncommon single and soar with You, to be all they were created to be. Amen!

Personal Daily Meditations for Singles

I Believe...
God's Plan Is Coming to Pass

Father, I thank You that You have a great plan for my life, and You are bringing it to pass in Your perfect timing. I refuse to worry or be discouraged, because You have started a good work in me, and You are faithful to complete it. You have not forgotten about me or changed Your mind about my divine destiny. I believe that You are ordering my steps and that I am walking out Your best plan for me. I know that all things are working together for my good because I love You, and I'm called according to Your purpose.

Scripture References

Jeremiah 29:11

Philippians 1:6

1 Thessalonians 5:24

Psalm 37:23

Romans 8:28

I BELIEVE...
MY JOY COMES FROM THE LORD

Father, You are the Source of my joy and security. I don't have to look to other people for fulfillment or happiness. The Greater One—Your Holy Spirit—lives in me, so every need in my life can be met, physically, emotionally, and spiritually. I bathe my spirit in Your Word so that I know who I am in Christ Jesus, and I am complete in Him. You are my light and my salvation and my strength!

Scripture References

Nehemiah 8:10

1 John 4:4

Colossians 2:10

Psalm 27:1

I BELIEVE...
I AM FREE FROM JEALOUSY AND FEAR

Thank You, Father, that as I delight myself in You, You are giving me the desires of my heart. I don't have to worry if others are being blessed, because I am being blessed, too! You are more than enough. I will not yield to jealousy, but will rejoice with others who are rejoicing. I resist jealousy and fear, and they must flee from me. I put the past behind and look to my future with faith. I won't be afraid of the future or see myself with anything but God's best for me. I can be content in this season of my life because of the promises in Your Word!

Scripture References

Psalm 37:4

James 4:7

2 Timothy 1:7

Philippians 4:11

I BELIEVE...
I AM A BLESSING AS
I FOCUS ON GOD

Father, thank You for helping me to fulfill the vision that You have placed in my heart. I am focusing my life on You. Put me in the right place at the right time with the right people doing the right thing. I want my life to bring You glory. I'll not be selfish or allow my thoughts and my actions to be focused only on myself, but I will reach out to be a blessing and a help to those around me. I will put my hand to what needs to be done, and I know that You will reward me and not forget my labor of love.

Scripture References

Acts 17:28

Deuteronomy 12:7

Hebrews 11:6

Hebrews 6:10

I BELIEVE...
MY WORDS HAVE POWER

Father, thank You for ordering the steps of my life. I will stay in agreement with You and keep my words in line with Your Word. I will speak words of faith over my life, because I understand that life and death are in the power of my tongue and I know that faith is how things change. I refuse to be caught in the trap of self-pity. I speak to discouragement and tell it to go, in Jesus' name. I call God's plan into my life, and I have whatsoever I say. I call those things which be not as though they were. I am full of joy by the words of my mouth!

Scripture References

Mark 11:23

Romans 4:17

Proverbs 18:21

1 John 5:4

I Believe...
I Will Marry the Right Person

Father, thank You that I am led by Your Spirit, and You will lead and guide me to the person I'm to spend the rest of my life with. All the good ones aren't taken—You have the right mate just for me! I commit my way to You, and I trust You to bring us together. I will be guided by Your peace, and I will also listen to the good advice of godly people around me. I hear Your voice clearly, and a stranger's voice I will not follow. I will not be unequally yoked together with an unbeliever. Thank You that as I pray and listen carefully to Your leading, the hidden things will be revealed. I believe that as I lean on, rely on, and trust in You, I will marry the right person!

Scripture References

Psalm 37:5

Colossians 3:15 AMP

Proverbs 1:5; 3:5,6; 11:14; 12:15

John 10:5

2 Corinthians 6:14

Mark 4:22

I BELIEVE...
I CAN ENJOY THIS
SEASON OF MY LIFE

Father, thank You that this is the day You have made, I will rejoice and be glad in it! My joy is in You, and You are working Your plan in perfect timing. I will take advantage of this season of being single and devote more time to You. I'll delight myself in seeking You, and I know You will reward me and give me the desires of my heart. I'll dedicate myself to being a blessing to others, and I know that when I help to make things happen for others, You can make things happen for me.

Scripture References

Psalm 118:24

Ecclesiastes 3:11

1 Corinthians 7:32-35

Psalm 37:4

Hebrews 11:6

Galatians 6:7

I BELIEVE...
GOD IS MOLDING
AND PREPARING ME

Father, I submit myself to Your hand. Mold me and prepare me for my future mate. Help me to become the best me I can be. I won't get anxious or in a hurry, but I will diligently apply myself to improving in the areas You show me I need to work on. Help me to grow spiritually and be committed to spiritual things so that You can complete the good work You have begun in me. Thank You for believing in me, Father, and for continuing to mold me into Your image every day.

Scripture References

Jeremiah 18:6

Philippians 4:6 AMP

Proverbs 10:4; 22:29

Ephesians 4:15

Philippians 1:6

2 Corinthians 3:18

I BELIEVE...
I CAN RESIST TEMPTATION

Father, when it comes to temptation in the area of sex, I declare that I am strong in You and the power of your might! I run away from fornication, in Jesus' name, just as Your Word says. I pray in the Spirit so that I will be built up and not enter into temptation. I will keep my body under. I feed my spirit regularly on the Word of God so that my resistance is strong. With a strong spirit I can cast down imaginations and thoughts that don't glorify You. As an act of my will, I set my mind on what is good, honest, pure, virtuous, and praiseworthy.

Scripture References

Ephesians 6:10

1 Corinthians 6:18

1 Corinthians 14:2

1 Corinthians 9:27

Matthew 26:41

2 Corinthians 5:10

Philippians 4:8

I BELIEVE...
GOD IS HELPING ME

Father, no matter what I'm going through, I know You are with me and You are helping me. Thank You that You will never fail me or leave me without support! My life is getting brighter and brighter, not dimmer and dimmer! Thank You for holding me up and letting me lean on You whenever I need comfort. I have nothing to fear because You are always with me and always strengthening me. You are my refuge and my fortress, and I confidently trust in Your help at all times.

Scripture References

Matthew 28:20

Hebrews 13:5 AMP

Proverbs 4:7,8

John 14:16-18

Isaiah 41:10 AMP

Psalm 91:2

I BELIEVE...
GOD'S LOVE IN ME NEVER FAILS

Father, thank You that everywhere I go today, Your love is in me, and it casts all fear out of my life. That love draws people to me and makes me a blessing everywhere I go. It keeps me and guards me. Because I am full of Your love, I am patient and kind today. I'm not proud or boastful or selfish. I'm not fretful, I don't hold a grudge, and I believe the best of everyone. Your love in me never, ever fails.

Scripture References

Romans 5:5

1 John 4:18

1 Corinthians 13:1-8 AMP

GOD'S WORD FOR
SUCCESSFUL SINGLES

God's Word for Successful Singles

Being confident of this very thing, that he which hath begun a good work in you will perform it until the day of Jesus Christ.

Philippians 1:6

Faithful is He who calls you, and He also will bring it to pass.

1 Thessalonians 5:24 NASB

And we know that all things work together for good to them that love God, to them who are the called according to his purpose.

Romans 8:28

Ye are of God, little children, and have overcome them: because greater is he that is in you, than he that is in the world.

1 John 4:4

The Lord is my light and my salvation; whom shall I fear? the Lord is the strength of my life; of whom shall I be afraid?

Psalm 27:1

...Resist the devil [stand firm against him], and he will flee from you.

James 4:7 AMP

Delight thyself also in the Lord; and he shall give thee the desires of thine heart.

Psalm 37:4

For God is not unrighteous to forget or overlook your labor and the love which you have shown for His name's sake in ministering to the needs of the saints (His own consecrated people), as you still do.

Hebrews 6:10 AMP

Death and life are in the power of the tongue: and they that love it shall eat the fruit thereof.

Proverbs 18:21

A man hath joy by the answer of his mouth....

Proverbs 15:23

The steps of a good man [or woman] are ordered by the Lord: and he delighteth in his way.

Psalm 37:23

But I would have you without carefulness. He that is unmarried careth for the things that belong to the Lord, how he may please the Lord:

But he that is married careth for the things that are of the world, how he may please his wife.

There is difference also between a wife and a virgin. The unmarried woman careth for the things of the Lord, that she may be holy both in body and in spirit: but she that is married careth for the things of the world, how she may please her husband.

And this I speak for your own profit; not that I may cast a snare upon you, but for that which is comely, and that ye may attend upon the Lord without distraction.

1 Corinthians 7:32-35

But seek ye first the kingdom of God, and his righteousness; and all these things shall be added unto you.

Matthew 6:33

…he that cometh to God must believe that he is, and that he is a rewarder of them that diligently seek Him.

Hebrews 11:6

Let us not give up meeting together, as some are in the habit of doing, but let us encourage one another—and all the more as you see the Day approaching.

Hebrews 10:25 NIV

He becometh poor that dealeth with a slack hand: but the hand of the diligent maketh rich.

Proverbs 10:4

I went by the field of the slothful, and by the vineyard of the man void of understanding;

And, lo, it was all grown over with thorns, and

nettles had covered the face thereof, and the stone wall thereof was broken down.

Then I saw, and considered it well: I looked upon it, and received instruction.

Yet a little sleep, a little slumber,

a little folding of the hands to sleep:

So shall thy poverty come as one that travelleth;

and thy want as an armed man.

Proverbs 24:30-34

There is that scattereth, and yet increaseth; and there is that withholdeth more than is meet, but it tendeth to poverty.

The liberal soul shall be made fat: and he that watereth shall be watered also himself.

Proverbs 11:24,25

The blessing of the Lord, it maketh rich, and he addeth no sorrow with it.

Proverbs 10:22

Seest thou a man diligent in his business? he shall stand before kings; he shall not stand before mean men.

Proverbs 22:29

Commit thy way unto the Lord; trust also in him; and he shall bring it to pass.

Psalm 37:5

...God, who quickeneth the dead, and calleth those things which be not as though they were.

Romans 4:17

And let the peace (soul harmony which comes) from Christ rule (act as umpire continually) in your hearts [deciding and settling with finality all questions that arise in your minds, in that peaceful state] to which as [members of Christ's] one body you were also called [to live]. And be thankful (appreciative), [giving praise to God always].

Colossians 3:15 AMP

Be ye not unequally yoked together with unbelievers: for what fellowship hath righteousness with unrighteousness? and what communion hath light with darkness?

2 Corinthians 6:14

Rebuke not an elder, but intreat him as a father; and the younger men as brethren;

The elder women as mothers; the younger as sisters, with all purity.

1 Timothy 5:1,2

"For there is nothing hidden which will not be revealed, nor has anything been kept secret but that it should come to light."

Mark 4:22 NKJV

...a man [or woman] of understanding shall attain unto wise counsels.

Proverbs 1:5

Where no counsel is, the people fall: but in the multitude of counsellors there is safety.

Proverbs 11:14

The way of a fool is right in his own eyes: but he that hearkeneth unto counsel is wise.

Proverbs 12:15

Flee fornication. Every sin that a man doeth is without the body; but he that committeth fornication sinneth against his own body.

1 Corinthians 6:18

*If we confess our sins, he [God] is faithful and just to forgive us
our sins, and to cleanse us from all unrighteousness.*

1 John 1:9

*And Jesus being full of the Holy Ghost returned from Jordan,
and was led by the Spirit into the wilderness,*

Being forty days tempted of the devil....

*And the devil said unto him, If thou be the Son of God,
command this stone that it be made bread.*

And Jesus answered him, saying, **It is written....**

Luke 4:1-4 (read vv. 1-13)

I also want women to dress modestly, with decency and propriety....

1 Timothy 2:9 NIV

*Watch and pray, that ye enter not into temptation: the spirit
indeed is willing, but the flesh is weak.*

Matthew 26:41

*For he that speaketh in an unknown tongue speaketh not unto
men, but unto God: for no man understandeth him; howbeit in the
spirit he speaketh mysteries.*

1 Corinthians 14:2

Likewise the Spirit also helpeth our infirmities....

Romans 8:26

*He who speaks in a [strange] tongue edifies and improves
himself....*

1 Corinthians 14:4 AMP

For with stammering lips and another tongue will he speak to this people.

To whom he said, This is the rest wherewith ye may cause the weary to rest; and this is the refreshing: yet they would not hear.

Isaiah 28:11,12

But I (Paul) keep under my body, and bring it into subjection: lest that by any means, when I have preached to others, I myself should be a castaway.

1 Corinthians 9:27

If you faint in the day of adversity, your strength is small.

Proverbs 24:10 AMP

but I say to you, that everyone who looks on a woman to lust for her has committed adultery with her already in his heart.

Matthew 5:28 NASB

Casting down imaginations, and every high thing that exalteth itself against the knowledge of God, and bringing into captivity every thought to the obedience of Christ.

2 Corinthians 10:5

...whatsoever things are true, whatsoever things are honest, whatsoever things are just, whatsoever things are pure, whatsoever things are lovely, whatsoever things are of good report; if there be any virtue, and if there be any praise, think on these things.

Philippians 4:8

...and, lo, I am with you alway, even unto the end of the world.

Matthew 28:20

...for He [God] Himself has said, I will not in any way fail you nor give you up nor leave you without support. [I will] not, [I will] not, [I will] not in any degree leave you helpless nor forsake nor let [you] down (relax My hold on you)! [Assuredly not!]

Hebrews 13:5 AMP

But the path of the righteous is like the light of dawn, that shines brighter and brighter until the full day.

Proverbs 4:18 NASB

And I will pray the Father, and he shall give you another Comforter, that he may abide with you for ever;

Even the Spirit of truth; whom the world cannot receive, because it seeth him not, neither knoweth him: but ye know him; for he dwelleth with you, and shall be in you.

I will not leave you comfortless: I will come to you.

John 14:16-18

"Do not be afraid; you will not suffer shame. Do not fear disgrace; you will not be humiliated. You will forget the shame of your youth and remember no more the reproach of your widowhood.

For your Maker is your husband...."

Isaiah 54:4,5 NIV

A man that hath friends must shew himself friendly....

Proverbs 18:24

Be ye not unequally yoked together with unbelievers: for what fellowship hath righteousness with unrighteousness? and what communion hath light with darkness?

2 Corinthians 6:14

Can two walk together, except they be agreed?

Amos 3:3

Love endures long and is patient and kind; love never is envious nor boils over with jealousy, is not boastful or vainglorious, does not display itself haughtily.

It is not conceited (arrogant and inflated with pride); it

is not rude (unmannerly) and does not act unbecomingly. Love (God's love in us) does not insist on its own rights or its own way, for it is not self-seeking; it is not touchy or fretful or resentful; it takes no account of the evil done to it [it pays no attention to a suffered wrong].

It does not rejoice at injustice and unrighteousness, but

rejoices when right and truth prevail.

Love bears up under anything and everything that comes, is ever ready to believe the best of every person, its hopes are fadeless under all circumstances, and it endures everything [without weakening].

Love never fails [never fades out or becomes obsolete or comes to an end]....

1 Corinthians 13:4-8 AMP

...let the wife see that she respects and reverences her husband [that she notices him, regards him, honors him, prefers him, venerates, and esteems him; and that she defers to him, praises him, and loves and admires him exceedingly].

Ephesians 5:33 AMP

[You are to feel for him all that reverence includes: to respect, defer to, revere him—to honor, esteem, appreciate, prize, and, in

the human sense, to adore him, that is, to admire, praise, be devoted to, deeply love, and enjoy your husband].

1 Peter 3:2 AMP

Endnotes

Chapter 1

[1] James E. Strong, "Greek Dictionary of the New Testament" in *Strong's Exhaustive Concordance of the Bible* (Nashville: Abingdon, 1890), p. 14, entry #573, S.V. "single," Matthew 6:22.

[2] Based on definitions from W. E. Vine, *An Expository Dictionary of New Testament Words,* (Old Tappan, New Jersey: Fleming H. Revell Company, 1966), p. 35, S.V. "SINGLE," "HAPLOUS," and "SINGLENESS," "I. APHELOTES."

[3] Definition based on Strong, "Hebrew and Chaldee Dictionary," p. 94, entry #6381, S.V. "singular."

[4] *Merriam-Webster OnLine Dictionary,* copyright © 2002, S.V. "single," and "SINGULAR"; available from <http://www.m-w.com>.

Chapter 2

[1] *The Geneva Bible,* "A facsimile of the 1560 edition" (Madison, Wisconsin: The University of Wisconsin Press, 1969), S.V. "Matthew 16:22."

[2] Based on a definition from W. E. Vine, p. 295, S.V. "REWARDER, MISTHAPODOTES."

Chapter 6

[1] Merriam-Webster, S.V. "flee."

[2] Based on a definition from Merriam-Webster, S.V. "fornication."

[3] Strong, "Main Concordance," p. 364, s.v. "fornication," "fornications," "fornicator," "fornicators."

[4] Based on a definition from Merriam-Webster, s.v. "adultery."

[5] Strong, "Main Concordance," p. 808, s.v. "pride."

[6] Ibid, pp. 536, 537, s.v. "jealous," "jealousy."

[7] Ibid, p. 982, s.v. "strife," "strifes."

[8] Ibid, pp. 701, 702, s.v. "murder," "murderer," "murderers," "murders."

[9] Ibid, p. 308, s.v. "envy," "envies," "envieth," "envying."

[10] Ibid, p. 285, s.v. "drunk," "drunkard," "drunkards," "drunken," "drunkenness."

[11] Ibid, pp. 599-600, 640, s.v. "liar," "liars," "lying."

[12] Ibid, pp. 975, 1032, s.v. "steal," "thief," "thieves."

[13] Ibid, p.18, s.v. "adulterers," "adulteress," "adulteresses," "adulteries," "adulterous," "adultery."

Chapter 7

[1] *International Standard Bible Encyclopedia,* Original James Orr 1915 Edition (Electronic Database: Biblesoft, 1995-1996), s.v. "EDIFICATION; EDIFY." All rights reserved.

[2] Ibid, s.v. "INFIRMITY."

Chapter 8

[1] "Are You Lonesome Tonight?" (RCA Victor, 1960), performed by Elvis Presley, words by Roy Turk, music by Lou Handman.

Chapter 10

[1] This does not mean that a woman should stay in an abusive situation. If a woman is being abused by her husband, she should seek help immediately!

An Important Message

If you have never met Jesus Christ, you can know Him today. God cares for you and wants to help you in every area of your life. That is why He sent Jesus to die for you. You can make your life right with God this very moment and make heaven your home.

Pray this prayer now:

Oh, God, I ask You to forgive me of my sins. I believe You sent Jesus to die on the cross for me. I receive Jesus Christ as my personal Lord and Savior. I confess Him as Lord of my life and I give my life to Him. Thank You, Lord, for saving me and for making me new. In Jesus' name, amen.

If you prayed this prayer, I welcome you to the family of God!

Please write to the address that follows and let me know about your decision for Jesus. I want to send you some free literature to help you in your new walk with the Lord.

To contact Kate McVeigh for book, tape,
ministry information, or for prayer, write:

Kate McVeigh Ministries
P.O. Box 1688
Warren, Michigan 48090
Or call: 1-800-40-FAITH (1-800-403-2484)

Or go online: www.katemcveigh.org

Please include your prayer requests and comments when you write.

Also, if you prayed this prayer to receive Jesus Christ as your Savior for the first time, please contact us on the web at www.harrisonhouse.com to receive a free book.

Or you may write to us at
Harrison House
P.O. Box 35035
Tulsa, Oklahoma 74153

About the Author

Rev. Kate McVeigh ministers extensively throughout the United States and abroad, preaching the Gospel of Jesus Christ with signs and wonders following. Her outreach ministry includes books, teaching tapes, a daily radio broadcast, "The Voice of Faith," as well as her weekly television broadcast, which airs throughout the United States.

Kate is known as a solid evangelist and teacher of the Gospel, with a powerful anointing to heal the sick and win the lost. Through Kate's down-to-earth and often humorous teaching of the Word, many are motivated to attain God's best for their lives.

Books by Kate McVeigh

The Blessing of Favor—
Experiencing God's Supernatural Influence

Sharing Your Faith:
Simple Steps to Lead Others to Christ

Additional copies of this book
are available from your local bookstore.

Experience God's Supernatural Influence

God's blessing of favor flowing in your life is not based upon your background, talents, abilities, or anything you have earned. It's God's promise to every believer from His Word, and all you have to do is receive it.

Kate McVeigh combines biblical truths with her own powerful testimony to illustrate how God's favor radically changed her from a timid, insecure girl into a woman full of strength and confidence. Learn how you too can expect your relationships, job, school, finances, and ministry to be filled with divine favor.

The Blessing of Favor
ISBN 978-1-57794-428-7

Fast. Easy.
Convenient.

For the latest Harrison House product information and author news, look no further than your computer. All the details on our powerful, life-changing products are just a click away. New releases, E-mail subscriptions, Podcasts, testimonies, monthly specials—find it all in one place. Visit harrisonhouse.com today!

harrisonhouse

The Harrison House Vision

Proclaiming the truth and the power

Of the Gospel of Jesus Christ

With excellence;

Challenging Christians to

Live victoriously,

Grow spiritually,

Know God intimately.